TWAYNE'S WORLD AUTHORS SERIES

A Survey of the World's Literature

Sylvia E. Bowman, Indiana University

GENERAL EDITOR

CHILE

John P. Dyson, Indiana University

EDITOR

Juan Godoy

(TWAS 189)

TWAYNE'S WORLD AUTHORS SERIES (TWAS)

The purpose of TWAS is to survey the major writers —novelists, dramatists, historians, poets, philosophers, and critics—of the nations of the world. Among the national literatures covered are those of Australia, Canada, China, Eastern Europe, France, Germany, Greece, India, Italy, Japan, Latin America, New Zealand, Poland, Russia, Scandinavia, Spain, and the African nations, as well as Hebrew, Yiddish, and Latin Classical literatures. This survey is complemented by Twayne's United States Authors Series and English Authors Series.

The intent of each volume in these series is to present a critical-analytical study of the works of the writer; to include biographical and historical material that may be necessary for understanding, appreciation, and critical appraisal of the writer and to present all material in clear, concise English—but not to vitiate the scholarly content of the work by doing so.

Juan Godoy

By THOMAS E. LYON
University of Wisconsin

Twayne Publishers, Inc. :: New York

Library of Congress Catalog Card Number: 73-161825

To Cheryl

Preface

In 1938 a new literary generation, led by an ambitious young professor of language, delivered the final blow to Chile's diehard Criollism. Twenty-six-year-old Juan Godoy defined the objectives of the generation and laboriously wrote his first novel, *Angurrientos* (*The Insatiable Ones*), a consummation of his literary theories. This new generation saw the literature of Mariano Latorre and other Criollist writers as mere depiction of human and telluric conduct, spatially organized on a horizontal plane. Criollist language, they felt, described objects and people much as a camera would capture them. Time was marginal to plot, which often became episodic.

Though not seeking the total defeat of Criollism, the young professor and his ambitious peers sought a deeper penetration of the soul of man, to discover the essence of culture and life. In Godoy's works, action moves in concentric circles, ignoring spatial progression. Language is a finely wrought stylistic device as well as a key to man's subconscious. The world is seen as behavior, not as a system of naturalistic determinations; and the man/nature complex is shown through a series of symbolic reiterations.

A student of Latorre for many years, a proud relative of Gabriela Mistral (Lucila *Godoy* Alcayaga), and the proclaimed leader of a generation which boasts of Nicomedes Guzmán, Fernando Algería, and Francisco Coloane, Godoy published novels and short stories from 1938 to 1968. Early in his career he was frequently hailed as capable of creating *the* Spanish-American novel, but in recent years his creative output has gradually slowed, and this expectation has not been realized.

This study will examine and appraise all of Juan Godoy's works in detail. Neither Godoy nor his generation have been studied in the United States; their treatment in Chile has been superficial. Due largely to the limited editions in which the author's novels have appeared, personally financed by him, only a few copies have reached libraries in the United States. Reprint editions are now beginning to appear which will rectify this situation. Godoy's teaching experience in philosophy and grammar provides a rich background for his works and the basis for the principal concepts of the study: analysis of Godoy's man-centered prose and an examination of style in language.

Preliminary investigations in both the United States and Chile have led to several conclusions which will here be analyzed: poetic intensification of narration, a strong rhythmic sense in prose, imagery and metaphor as the basis for depicting the created world, man governed by feelings rather than by reason, a spiritual relationship between man and the natural world, and rich and varied narrative techniques. The total effect is a prose which transcends nationalistic limitations and achieves lasting, universal stature.

All translations are my own.

THOMAS E. LYON

Contents

Acknowledgments

Special acknowledgment is made to the National Endowment for the Humanities for their Summer Stipend, 1968. Funds provided by said office permitted quiet research into the prose of Juan Godoy and criticism relating to his works. Appreciation is likewise expressed to John A. Crow and Ricardo Benavides who read the original manuscript.

Chronology

1911   June 7: Juan Godoy born in Chillán, Chile, fifty-five miles northeast of Concepción. Only son of Juan Antonio Godoy and Elisa Corbalán de Godoy.

1913   Family moved to Ancud, island town off coast of southern Chile.

1918   Family moved to Antofagasta, port town in northern Chile. Primary School and two years in the Lyceum of Antofagasta.

1925   Family moved to Santiago, capital and cultural center. Valentín Letelier Lyceum; studied with the famous Criollist writer Mariano Latorre.

1931   Graduated from Santiago's renowned Lastarria Lyceum.

1932   Student in the Pedagogical Institute of the University of Chile, studying Spanish literature and grammar. Studied under Yolando Pino Saavedra, César Búnster, Rodolfo Oroz, Ricardo Latcham, and, again, Mariano Latorre.

1933   April 2: Married Regina Astica Fuentes.

1934   Named assistant (instructor) in modern grammar in the Pedagogical Institute.

1936   Elected president of the student organization of the Pedagogical Center, an activist organization. Participated in musical and dramatic presentations.

1938   Graduated from the Pedagogical Institute, with a thesis entitled "Grammatical Categories and Their Relationship with Logical and Psychological Categories." Completion and circulation of manuscript copy of first novel, *Angurrientos* (*The Insatiable Ones*). Political activity in the Popular Front party and direct participation in the presidential election of Pedro Aguirre Cerda. First teaching position, in Santiago's prestigious National Institute, to 1960; simultaneous appointment in the National School of Graphic Arts.

1940   Publication of ·*Angurrientos*.

1941   Publication of "La lengua del buey" ("The Ox Tongue").

1945   Publication of *La cifra solitaria* (*The Lonely Cipher*), second major novel.

1948   Treatment in an institution for alcoholics.

1950   Publication of "Un inspector de sanidad. . . . o como un alto dignatario murió en sus manos" ("A Public Health Inspector. . . . Or, How an Important Dignitary Died in His Hands").

1952 *El gato de la maestranza y otros cuentos* (*Cat in the Round-house and Other Stories*).

1955 Preached funeral sermon of Mariano Latorre.

1959 Publication of *Sangre de murciélago* (*Bat's Blood*).

1960 Member of the faculty of the State Technical University in Santiago; to the present.

1962 Death of mother and wife.

1963 Recipient of Peoples National Literary Prize for his prose writings.

1968 Publication of short novel *El impedido* (*The Invalid*).

CHAPTER 1

Juan Godoy–"A Vital Desire for Life"

THE Chilean critic Ricardo A. Latcham calls Juan Godoy "the most interesting of the contemporary authors"[1] and refers to him as "perhaps the best of the native stylists."[2] Juan Loveluck, another critic of the Latin American novel, adds that "of his entire generation, Godoy is the most gifted";[3] Raúl Morales Alvarez goes even further in his praise when he states, "Godoy represents—alone—a whole generation."[4] Juan Godoy—Chilean author, lauded by critics of his country, virtually unknown to the rest of the world.

Born June 7, 1911, this only son was softly pampered by two older sisters. For the first year and a half of his life the family lived in the small agricultural town of Chillán, fifty-five miles northeast of Concepción.

The author's father, Juan Antonio Godoy, director-composer for a military band in the province of Ñuble, brought a sense of rhythm and an appreciation of music into the home. The senior Godoy at one time created an opera, never published, but now cherished by Juan as one of the few tangible memories of his father,[5] who died tragically when the son was only fourteen.

Godoy frequently mentions his great-aunt, Gabriela Mistral, Nobel Prize winner (1945), his paternal grandfather's sister, whose true name, Lucila Godoy Alcayaga, links her directly to the novelist. Juan Godoy feels a deep pride in this relationship and frequently points out a spiritual unity between Gabriela's poetry and his own poetic prose.

Contrary to the short, agitated life of his father, Godoy's mother was the everpresent, calming influence in his life. Of rural parentage, Elisa Corbalán absorbed the rich narrative, legendary tales of rural Chile and passed them on to her only son as he requested bedtime stories. From her lips Juan Godoy heard many of the legends and popular stories he would later intercalate in his novels. The picaresque story of the Negro Faci-

13

quillo in *Angurrientos* (*The Insatiable Ones*) is a derivative of the Chilean oral tradition. *Angurrientos* is dedicated to Godoy's mother, a further indication of her influence upon him.

When non-Catholic missionary activity increased in southern Chile, Elisa became an evangelist. She purchased a large, illustrated Bible for the family, from which she read to her three children, instilling in them a love for the poetic narrative of the Scriptures. Much of the religious symbolism of Godoy's *La cifra solitaria* (*The Lonely Cipher*) can be traced to his early evangelistic exposure to the Bible.

After the death of her husband in 1926, Elisa Corbalán de Godoy struggled to keep her family together, living with her married daughters, and finally with Juan during the last twenty-eight years of her life. One critic, describing Godoy's house and family, states: "In that house Juan Godoy, his aged mother with her snowy hair and perpetual, homey smile live. . . ."[6] She died in Santiago in 1962.

The profound influence of Godoy's parents and ancestors upon his life and works is undeniable. He personally expresses that with such a famous great-aunt he felt compelled to write. His father brought rhythm and music into his life, while his mother instilled in him a feeling for the narrative, popular aspects of literature.

In 1913 his father was transferred to the tiny island-town of Ancud. The seashore became a backyard playground for three-year-old Juan. Although it might be argued that the boy was too young to remember these scenes of early childhood, he claims a vivid recollection of them, as seen in *Sangre de murciélago* (*Bat's Blood*), where one of the main characters recalls various incidents from his childhood: a deep well behind his house which gives him vertigo, a boat trip from the island to the mainland, his dog Plutón, fear of the giant blue-tailed flies. Even more astonishing about his childhood is Godoy's insistence that he recalls an event which occurred six months before he was born— the appearance of Halley's comet. In an interview on November 17, 1966, Juan strongly maintained that he remembered the occurrence and the fear it caused him as well as the entire population—not from photographs but from witnessing the phenomenon. He believes that he was able to see through his mother's eyes, in some metaphysical way, while still inside her womb.

One definite result of the nearly three years the family lived in the island and port atmosphere is the role of the sea in numerous tropes and metaphors appearing in novels having little or nothing to do with the sea. It is evident that these memories were deep and living and that they flowered from the depths of his subconsciousness as precious childhood images that grow inadvertently as the man grows. In addition to honoring his mother in his first novel, he dedicates it to: "My land—which is like a great furrow of waves . . ." (first edition, p. 3).

In 1918, when Juan was seven, the family moved again, this time to the seaport of Antofagasta in northern Chile. In Antofagasta, a larger, more metropolitan town than any he had previously known, Juan began his formal schooling. Advancing rapidly, he completed primary school in four years and entered the Lyceum of Antofagasta, where he studied for two years. The Godoys then left the north with its impressive mountains for the noisy streets of Santiago.

Juan began his third year of humanities in Santiago's Valentín Letelier Lyceum in 1925. Here Mariano Latorre whetted his poetic appetite with the beauty and grace of the Spanish language and its literature. His sixth and final year was spent in the famous Lastarria Lyceum, where he was graduated in 1931.

During this period, following the death of his father, Juan's family lived on the outskirts of Santiago, near the General Cemetery. Little money was available, and the family's living conditions gradually worsened. Being a newcomer to the capital, Juan had few friends outside his humble family. Under these circumstances, bordering on poverty, Juan found inspiration for the brooding, solitary, ever hungry characters that grace his novels. With the conviction that education was the only answer to his own temporal anxieties, in 1932 he entered the Pedagogical Institute of the University of Chile. With his characteristic superexuberance and overestimation of himself, Godoy chose to study French and Spanish simultaneously. After an exhausting first year—unable to meet the demands of the two fields—he dropped French, and gave his full attention to his first love—Spanish Literature.

In his first year in the institute he met and courted Regina Astica Fuentes, a sixteen-year-old girl of Basque parentage. The courtship was carried on in secret because of the traditional pride of Regina's parents who forbade her to associate with a young student from so poor a family. Juan became increasingly persistent and almost daily composed verses and poetic love letters for his sweetheart. Finally, on April 2, 1933, on the advice of his mother, but without the knowledge of Regina's parents, Juan Godoy rented a horse-drawn taxi and secreted his lover away to be married. She was seventeen; he, twenty-one. Regina lovingly saved Juan's letters through the years; they are still in existence, and Juan often dreams of basing a romantic novel on their contents.

Godoy continued in the Pedagogical Institute where he was an excellent student and soon was named assistant in modern grammar. At the university he was exposed to many of the outstanding writers and critics of Chile. Yolando Pino Saavedra, who instructed Godoy in esthetics, as well as in style and composition, recalls Juan as an eager student who excelled both in literature and in language study, a rare achievement among his colleagues.[7]

In 1936 Juan Godoy was elected president of the Pedagogical Center and from then on began to exercise his personal influence over the young artists in the same institution. With a few other students, mostly from his own field of Spanish literature, he formed an Aphonic Orchestra in which the members dressed in absurd, outdated costumes and performed "aphonic music"— music with no rhythm or reason. The experiences with that group remain among the fondest memories of Godoy's university years. From that nucleus, according to Juan, sprang the theater of Pedro de la Barra, which evolved into Chile's present Experimental Theater.

The year 1938 is perhaps the most significant in the life of Juan Godoy. He completed his thesis and was graduated from the Pedagogical Institute. The thesis carries the complex title, "Grammatical Categories and Their Relationship with Logical and Psychological Categories," and is an indication of Godoy's compelling concern for language, its usage, and its relationship to philosophy. Indeed, the title he received, Professor of Spanish and Philosophy, cannot be fully understood without an examination of the thesis. The bibliography includes a few basic grammatical studies but draws more heavily from philosophical works and early texts in psychology. The work itself is a monument to the erudition, meditation, and dedication of Juan Godoy. Juan worked on his thesis writing in the late evening and early morning hours; his wife did the typing during the day with the questionable help of two small children.

During this same year Juan also finished the manuscript for his first novel, *Angurrientos.* He had presented the idea for the novel to friends—Fernando Alegría, Mariano Latorre, Nicomedes Guzmán, and others—and with their encouragement, completed and circulated a typewritten copy in November, 1938. So popular was the manuscript that when it was finally published in 1940, Juan Godoy had already received more than thirty letters of congratulation from some of the foremost critics in Chile. From these letters he selected comments by Mariano Latorre, Ricardo A. Latcham, and Alberto Romero to grace the inside jacket flaps of the first edition, thus creating the misleading impression that the volume was a second edition.

Since early 1937 Juan Godoy, as a student leader, had been actively working for the rising political party, the Popular Front. In 1938, the party's Pedro Aguirre Cerda was elected president of the country, signifying the rise of a new nationalism-socialism in Chile. Godoy took pride in the role he had played in that victory.

With a completed education, a title, some political experience, and a novel in manuscript, Juan Godoy was ready in 1938 to begin his life's work as professor of Spanish. In the same significant year, he accepted a job in the National Institute, at that time the most prestigious secondary school in Chile. There, with César Búnster, Roberto Prada, Oscar Marín, Mario Osses, and other critics and writers, he was to write the succeeding novels and short stories that brought him fame. In buildings located directly behind the University of Chile, Godoy was near the pulse of intellectual trends of the day. César Búnster, also a professor of Spanish, relates how Godoy would often come to him with a new short story or chapter from a novel and say, "Try this out on your class; tell them it's from a young Chilean writer, and get their reaction." Búnster complied with his friend's desires and found that his students generally received the fragments very well.[8] For twenty-two years, from 1938 to 1960, Godoy continued to teach at the National Institute.

While teaching at the National Institute, Godoy also gave classes in the National School of Graphic Arts, a position which would prove a boon to the young man with ideas, plans, and manuscripts. It was here, in 1940, that he oversaw the publication of *Angurrientos,* and later another novel and two volumes of short stories. He finally had a publisher—himself. Occasionally, Juan Godoy gave classes in the night school, Federico Hanssen, to supplement his meager income from the National Institute. The financial status of his family improved enough that during these years he was able to fulfill a dream of many middle-class Chileans—he constructed and grew a grapevine arbor. The backyard of his home, under the shady arbor, became a gathering place for many of Chile's leading artists. Juan would often entertain the group with the popular national songs of the times, singing in his nasal bass voice and accompanying himself on his guitar.

During the first few years in the National Institute, events occurred which changed both the life and the literary production of Juan Godoy. He began to drink, first on social occasions, and then in the numerous bars of Santiago. This one "tiny vice" has probably been the biggest single influence in Godoy's adult life. As a young writer he was hailed as Chile's outstanding novelist, capable of producing *the* novel of Chile or America;[9] as a mature adult, he is avoided and forgotten, left with his dreams and destructive wine. Many literary critics, and even relatives, have pointed up the duality in Godoy's person; he has the ability and desire to be a truly great writer, and yet he destroys the possibility of writing by losing his thoughts and plans in alcohol.

When his drinking problem became critical, Godoy's sister-in-law, María Astica Fuentes, a social worker, persuaded him to enter an institution for alcoholics. Euphemistically christened with the English name El Open Door, and located in the hills southeast of Santiago, the institution accepts drug addicts and psychotics as well as alcoholics. During two and a half months of the summer vacation (January-March, 1948), Godoy was voluntarily confined for treatments, or so his family thought. After the period was over it was discovered that he had elusively avoided treatment by making friends with the doctors and assisting them in their duties among the psychotics, thus avoiding any disagreeable treatments himself.

Most relatives of Juan Godoy do not consider him an alcoholic; they prefer the term "dipsomaniac," explaining that he may completely forget wine for a month or more, and then suddenly develop an uncontrollable craving. They regard his drinking as an innocent, nearly spontaneous act; there is no stigma attached to it. In fact, it has even been interpreted as a true representation of Chilean life: "Godoy is the audacious mental adventure of all Chile, its illusions and failures; the unfurled sail of hope, the catastrophe breaking on the coast, resting in the arms of Apollo or the flute of Dionysus."[10]

With the exception of his eldest son, Godoy's children were born during his early years of teaching. Juan Ariel was born in 1934 while his father was still a student. Elisa, named for the novelist's mother, was born in 1938, and is now married to one of Chile's brilliant young poets, Waldo Rojas. María Fresia was born in 1942, and Pedro in 1946.

Although Juan Godoy has enjoyed a long career as a professor of Spanish, he considers himself first an artist and second a teacher. Teaching is necessary, since his writing has never proved lucrative; but the demands of this "second profession" left him limited time for travel. The boundaries of his geographical world are those of Chile, and he has not traveled extensively in his own country.

In 1962 Juan's white-haired mother died, and a few months later he also lost his wife of thirty years, Regina. This left the man more alone than ever, and his home disintegrated. Without Regina's thoughtful care many of his books were borrowed and never returned, and his personal library became scattered. Valuable first editions of his novels were lost. In recent years his kindly sister-in-law, María Astica Fuentes, has set aside a room for him in her home in the San Miguel section of Santiago.

Only in recent years have Godoy and his works begun to win acclaim. Second editions of two of his novels were published, at small expense to the author. *Angurrientos* was reprinted in 1959; *La cifra solitaria*, in 1962. In September, 1963, Godoy was awarded the Peoples' National Prize for his contributions to Chilean literature. He was nominated for the country's highest prize, the National Prize for Literature, in 1966, but failed to receive this award. Godoy has again been nominated for this honor and may yet receive it. Many critics, such as the influential Mario Ferrero, favor Godoy's selection: "On more than one occasion I have been asked who would be my selection for the next National Prize for Literature. . . . In prose I would say Alberto Romero, Daniel Belmar, and especially, Juan Godoy."[11]

Godoy is extremely introspective, and his inner thoughts and desires frequently stimulate spontaneous bursts of poetry. Often, without the slightest visual or sensorial provocation, he will break into verse, reciting almost without error Lope, Quevedo, Góngora, or some other Golden Age poet; occasionally it will be a French symbolist, a fragment of a poem in Latin, or Poe's "Annabel Lee." He rarely talks of his past life but often of the future and his plans for fame and further creation. Through drink he finds a certain identification with the masses, the *pueblo*, of which he desires to be a part, though he still maintains an intellectual awareness of his superiority. His many years as a student and professor of literature have provided opportunities to read, compare, and enjoy many authors in many literatures. Edgar Allan Poe and William Faulkner are his favorite North American writers. Swift's *Gulliver's Travels* and the poetry of John Donne rank in his mind as England's highest accomplishments. The great Russian novelists Gorki, Andreyev, and Dostoevski, are constantly quoted and compared. Gerard de Nerval's prose is one of Godoy's great loves, and he feels an artistic union with this nineteenth-century Frenchman. The Spanish Golden Age writers, many unfamiliar to the ordinary student, are also vital to Godoy. All of the above-mentioned writers have had their influence on Juan Godoy, molding and influencing his mind and literature.

Juan Godoy is known mainly for four novels, one collection of short stories, and frequent stories published in magazines, bulletins, and anthologies.

In chronological sequence, *Angurrientos* is the first of these works. It was first published in 1940, though written in 1937 and 1938, but it was widely circulated in manuscript form in the interim. The two-year delay was due to the lack of a publisher and the high cost of printing. Juan was twenty-six years old and still a student while writing his initial novel. Simultaneously, he was writing his thesis on grammatical categories. The relationship between that thesis and his literary works can be seen in his careful use of words and tropes. The conditions of poverty in which Juan Godoy lived as a student provided the inspiration and background for the novel; he interpreted his environment in terms of literary figures and ideas. Remembering the genesis of the work, Godoy has said: "My first novel, *Angurrientos*, occurred to me from a vague desire to write. So many men, sufferings, and scenes that beat against my soul. I had never written previously. The context came to me in the form of a short story and so I fashioned a novel. Many lives agitate throughout these pages and a great love for our Chile."[12]

His teaching position at the National School of Graphic Arts provided the funds for the low-cost publication of the well-worn manuscript. Before going to press, however, Godoy again reread the typewritten copy and made at least 150 minor corrections. This writer had the opportunity of examining the manuscript, counting and analyzing the corrections. The most important changes are those which affect the rhythm and sound of the sentence, an indication that the manuscript was read aloud for correction—the addition of commas to break up the sentence and give a sense of rhythm; *pero* (the more prosaic form of "but") is often changed to *mas*, giving a more poetic tone to the narration; verbal compliments are shifted in position to more perfectly complete the rhythm of the sentence. Godoy underlined many words and metaphors, undoubtedly intending to rework the copy once again but apparently was unable to do so. He was never completely satisfied in his attempt to achieve lyric perfection in this first novel.

The book is dedicated to his mother and to his country, the "great furrow of waves." A sketch of Godoy by Israel Roa and a ninety-one-word glossary of difficult regionalistic terms, compiled by Godoy himself, are included in the volume. The glossary was added after several friends had read the manuscript; the author realized that many of his words would not be understood by those unexposed to the "Angurrientism" of Chilean life.

In November, 1940, Godoy selected and paid for the type, the paper, and the cover for the novel, and he oversaw the printing, which was handled by three of his students. In December, 1940, 480 copies were completed. Some were distributed for sale, but the majority were given to friends, critics, and relatives. Juan Godoy does not recall receiving any money from the sale of the book, although it was quickly sold out. Within a month *Atenea, Acción Social, Los Libros Por Dentro, Boletín del Instituto Nacional, La Nación,* and *Hoy* had reviewed the novel; all were favorable, even laudatory. Several critics pointed to a direct influence from Gabriel Miró, but Godoy sees the relationship as a stylistic coincidence, since he had not read the Spaniard's works until after the comparisons were made.

Even before its publication, the novel had become the ideo-

logical basis and password for a new generation in Chile known
as *Angurrientismo*. Juan Godoy was the acknowledged leader,
as a result of the novel and of two critical articles, "Satiety and
Culture" and "Short Essay on the Common Man," which will be
discussed in subsequent chapters.

Although admired and read by critics and other writers,
Godoy was still unknown to the masses. This is obvious in the
fact that, although the few copies of the first edition of *Angurrientos* were completely sold out in 1941, it was 1959 before the
publishing house Nascimento printed a second edition of two
thousand copies. All these copies quickly sold to literary critics,
professors, and students. The second edition contained no addi-
tions or corrections to the body of the novel. It had however,
a new illustrated jacket, and the blurb on the inside was even
more eulogistic than that in the first edition. The new printing
also brought many more reviews and set off a reevaluation of
Godoy's contributions to Chilean literature.

Five tormented years after his first, Godoy's second novel appeared. In the National School of Graphic Arts he had made
friends with Israel Roa, one of Chile's leading painters and
sketchers. Knowing of Godoy's narrative ability and desire to
discover and reveal "Chilean cultural essence," Roa told him
of a blind man living in the little town of Angol, 380 miles to
the south of Santiago, and suggested that Godoy visit the town
and the man to gather narrative material. After a train ride
of a day and a night, Godoy found only deserted streets in the
town of Angol, no dramatic elements for a novel, and was informed that the blind man had recently died. Undaunted, the
young writer stayed for several days, taking notes and recording
impressions, feelings, and characterizations. To these observations he added a short piece of poetic prose written in 1941,
"The Ox Tongue"; then, by creating the blind man he had never
known, and adding a little of his own childhood, Godoy wrote
La cifra solitaria.

In November, 1945, a thousand-copy edition of this second
novel was published, again by the students of the Graphic Arts
School. Israel Roa effectively illustrated the front of the jacket
with a color picture of the blind protagonist, and appropriately
integrated four other black-and-white sketches, depicting scenes
from the novel. In order to execute his sketches accurately, Roa
read the manuscript prior to its publication. The novel is ded-

icated to: "Israel Roa and César Búnster, gentlemen from Angol." Both were Godoy's colleagues, Roa in Graphic Arts and Búnster in the National Institute. Búnster had assisted Godoy by reading parts of the typescript to his literature classes. Roa had suggested the locale. *La cifra solitaria* received favorable reviews, similar to those of the first novel, in the leading journals and papers of Chile. Even the small-town paper of Angol, *El Esfuerzo,* obliged with a front-page review on December 22, 1945. In a short time the title began appearing in book lists, followed by the familiar "sold out." As with the first novel, a few copies found their way to some university libraries in the United States: University of California at Los Angeles and at Berkeley, Harvard, University of Illinois at Urbana, and a few others. Most were purchased or given away in Chile.

Despite the laudatory nature of the reviews, the book was not reprinted until 1962, when the National School of Graphic Arts published an edition of 1,150 copies, also financed by Godoy. The title is altered slightly, from *La cifra solitaria* to *Cifra solitaria.* Gone are the drawings by Israel Roa, as well as the dedication to Roa and Búnster. A few copies of this edition are still available, mostly from the author.

In 1950, Graphic Arts published a single short story with the lengthy title of "A Public Health Inspector.... Or, How an Important Dignitary Died in His Hands(*)", with the footnote at the bottom of the jacket explaining: "(*) Not *by* His Hands Because the Inspector Didn't Kill Him." The title itself indicates the sarcastic tone of the story, which pans a high government official whose most important work is explaining obvious details. Roa has once again drawn several sketches illustrating a few of the thirty pages. The work contains no dedicatory statement as did the first two books. This thousand-copy edition was also printed at the author's expense. A listing of the author's works on an inside page informs the reader that a book of short stories, *El gato de la maestranza* (*Cat in the Roundhouse*), and a novel, *Sangre de murciélago,* would soon be published. The short stories appeared two years later; the novel was delayed nine.

Owing to shortage of funds and a lack of renown in his own country, no publishing house was willing to risk publication of Godoy's short stories. Hence, in 1952 Graphic Arts loyally published one thousand copies of the 130-page *El gato de la maestranza* and Israel Roa provided illustrations. The collection includes a chapter from *Angurrientos*, the already published "Inspector," and several as yet unpublished short stories. There are dedications to Agustín Venegas and Humberto Beltramín, personal friends of the author.

In an essay explaining his method of literary creation, Godoy has stated that his starting point for both novel and short story is always an image, seen or conceived instantaneously. From this image, or series of images in the case of a novel, he creates the work. This spontaneous technique in Godoy's creations parallels more the inspiration of a poet than a novelist, as was noted by critics, perhaps before Godoy himself was even aware of it: "Juan Godoy, author of *Angurrientos* and *La cifra solitaria* writes little, even appearing to avoid writing. But it is not he who calls forth the work, rather, the completed work springs forth impetuously from its father, Godoy, as Athena from Zeus's head."[13]

As previously indicated, the novel *Sangre de murciélago* was proposed as early as 1950 but was not completed and published until 1959. It is based on the personal experience of the author in the "Open Door" during 1948. It was recorded in fragments, on notebooks, inside book covers, on anything the author could find. From these notes and commentary recorded in 1948, Godoy fashioned a novel. He began in 1952; the following year he submitted the second chapter to a short-story contest but was unsuccessful. By 1955 the narrative was in its final form, and the manuscript was read by several friends. But not until 1959 did Godoy find a publisher. No longer a member of the faculty of Graphic Arts, he had to find other contacts. Finally the small Prensa Latinoamericana published this novel, Godoy's favorite, in an edition of two thousand copies. The cover jacket is illustrated not by Roa but by Mariano Díaz; there is no dedicatory statement. Godoy appears here to have purposely disassociated himself from his old friends and contacts. For the first time in his writing experience he simply surrendered the manuscript to a publisher and had no further say over its appearance. The published novel curiously contains a short biographical sketch on the author and a three-page bibliography prepared as part of a thesis done on Godoy in the Pedagogical Institute of the University of Chile. Godoy himself submitted these two items as part of the manuscript.

During the four years Godoy pondered and planned *Sangre de murciélago,* and the three years of actual writing (1952-55), he read much background material. Jack London's biography excited him. C. R. Jackson's *Lost Weekend* provided a literary example after which Godoy could fashion his creation. He read several medical treatises on alcoholism. But, according to Godoy's own explanation, the book *Psychoanalysis of the Writer* by Edmund Belger, first published in Spanish in 1954, had the deepest influence on his writing. After reading Belger he began, even more freely, to examine his own life through literature. He created two main characters, the narrator and the sculptor, who actually represent the same person, Juan Godoy. By splitting himself in two, he could better examine his own actions. When questioned as to the nature and identity of the two protagonists, Godoy sorrowfully stated: "At the end of the story, where I allowed the sculptor to be killed, I amputated half of myself."[14] Unable to understand the meaning of one of the dreams in the the novel, this writer inquired of Godoy, who brushed the question aside with, "Neither do I understand it; it is merely a dream that I had during that time [of writing the novel]; it has some meaning." As these two statements evidence, the life of the author is richly woven into the novel. The work does not attempt to be autobiographical, but rather is a novelized re-creation of some of Godoy's life experiences. He would like this novel to be better known and understood because "into it I threw my whole self," he says.

Fifteen of the journals and newspapers of Chile immediately reviewed this personalized novel, most very favorably, and *Sangre de murciélago* rapidly joined the sold-out list. No second edition has appeared, but the author speaks of reediting it for another printing in the near future. He is desirous of having the novel translated and published abroad, since he feels it has universal appeal.

Since 1959, Godoy has only written one short story, "Sombras" ("Shadows"), a type of last memorial to his patient wife, and a short novel. He has the plots for two more novels worked out in his mind, but lacks the tranquility or discipline to actually write them. *El impedido (The Invalid)* was written in 1968 and relates in depth the psychological turmoil of a worker, temporarily crippled, who provides a lover for his too easily excitable wife during his convalescence. It was published with the aid of the municipality of San Miguel, a suburb of Santiago, in an edition of 1,150 copies, by Ediciones Quenaci, in 1968. It is described as a *nouvelle* by the author, containing sixty-two pages. Once again, Godoy's work was illustrated by Israel Roa and an introduction was provided by Jorge Jobet.

An obvious conclusion from the above is that Juan Godoy's writing is not extensive. A few novels, a few short stories, and a little criticism constitute the sum total of his creative work. Reasons for his parsimony are many. Primary might be alcohol, which in some degree may heighten literary creation but in excess inhibits and dams that creation. Godoy has existed in an agitated, perpetual-motion kind of life and has not enjoyed the serenity conducive to creativity. His style is a difficult, involved one, and his perfectionistic desires drive him to cross out, add, redo, check, and rework. His method of writing, as critics have shown, is not orderly, but often jumbled and chaotic. Perhaps foremost, his own confession, "I have to suffer, suffer deeply, before writing,"[15] is the most satisfying explanation. He suffers through long hours of preparation and tedious development of images, ideas, plots, and characters. He suffers in his struggle for perfection of each word, line, and sentence. The writing and rewriting process brings added suffering. In short, the demands he makes of himself have limited the quantity but have enhanced the quality of his literature. His limited output is one of the chief reasons he has not received Chile's National Prize for Literature.[16] Almost without exception his reviewers conclude their brief essays with a plea for more of Godoy: "He [Godoy] places Chilean narrative on a superior plane, bringing it to the sphere of potential creative greatness. We hope that the author will give us many more pages of such extraordinary and meaningful content."[17]

A second factor in Godoy's lack of popularity has been the scarcity of his volumes. All were printed in small editions, even according to publishing standards in Chile. The few copies that made their way to bookstores were quickly sold; and reprints, until recently, have not been available. This meant that students of Chilean literature would likely hear about Juan Godoy but be unable to read his works. The problem is even more acute in the United States, where only a few universities have been able to obtain copies of his works, mainly as gifts from Chilean faculty members. In Chile, bookstore owners have heard of Juan Godoy, but few have acquired or read his novels. The small editions of the four works originally printed by Graphic Arts kept Godoy out of the circle of recognition. Costs of publication came from his own pocket, so that he could only afford small printings; small printings brought no fame or money; consequently, the next new volume was also destined to a small printing; and so on. Godoy himself has jealously kept all copyright powers and, for unknown reasons, did not grant permission to the Nascimento for a reprint of *Angurrientos* until 1959. He has had no publisher who would push his works for the sake of profit, and therefore bring recognition to the author. His novels appeared in no catalogs, and if Graphic Arts was unable to distribute them, Godoy simply took them home to a forgotten bookshelf.

Godoy is relatively unknown, not for literary reasons, but for extraliterary ones. His critics have been almost overly favorable about the quality of his works; his work is good. But his personal life and the small, undistributed editions of his creations have been the factors which, to many, make him just one more name in Spanish-American literature. Even in Chile he is unstudied (except for the 1955 thesis already mentioned). There is much evidence, however, that this situation is changing, in Chile and in the United States.

On the back jacket of the 1940 edition of *Angurrientos*, centered and neatly framed, appear the words: "A movement dedicated to the intuition of Chilean cultural essence." Godoy wrote a type of manifesto for the movement, personally influenced many young artists to follow the new wave, and claimed for himself the leadership of a generation. Neither *La cifra solitaria, Sangre de murciélago,* nor his short stories carry a tag identifying them with "Angurrientism"—this movement directed toward revealing "cultural essence"—but for the purpose of the present study, Godoy's works will be considered as a whole. This is not to say that all his works are part of the "Angurrientist" movement; they could not be so classified. But all show an obvious attempt to penetrate and elucidate, often poetically, certain aspects of life in Chile. The totality of the works is superior to the style, technique, or *school* of any single one of them. In subsequent chapters, as style and themes are examined, any differences between the works will be immediately apparent, but each work will not be dissected and discussed separately. No attempt should be made to divide the life or works of Godoy into sections or periods.

It is hoped that this brief sketch of Godoy's life and the study of bibliographical details will lead to richer enjoyment and understanding of his works. It is intended only as background for, not as a key for, interpretation of his works; only a detailed study of the works themselves can achieve effective interpretation. This initial section has examined a life, not a fictional creation: "And this is Juan Godoy, man and boy, tormented and serene, bright and baroque, just a step away from great literature, from the masterful and unforgettable. If wine does not destroy his body, his spiritual light will illuminate Hispanic América."[18]

I   Juan Godoy in the Generation of 1938

That Chile experienced a change in literary climate and kind around 1938 can be little disputed. Grouped around the victory of the Popular Front party and the election of Pedro Aguirre Cerda as president, a group of young activist writers emerged and united under the direction of Juan Godoy. As a student leader in the University of Chile, Godoy aligned himself with the new coalition Popular Front party and assisted in the 1938 victory. The date was epecially important to young artists concerned with the masses, who now felt an alliance with the government and its ambitions, a closeness they had previously not experienced. They rallied together under Godoy, united in an attitude of triumph, feeling that the country was taking a fortuitous turn. The pessimism and anger which characterized most of Spain's artists and intellectuals after 1936 was reversed in Chile with the victory of the Popular Front. Writers walked the slippery ground of social criticism, not in the political, but in the human aspect. This simple factor gave unity to their ambitions and their works and solidified a generation.

The suggested 1938 date for this generation does not follow the neat scheme devised by José Juan Arrom, who would impose upon all Hispanic-American letters the uniform pattern of a new generation arising in 1924 and ending in 1954.[19] He calls this period one of Vanguardism and Post-Vanguardism, terms that convey little meaning for the objectives of Chile's recognized generation of 1938. The year 1938 falls almost exactly in the middle of Arrom's thirty-year generation and must be considered what he calls the "Second promotion." Arrom's system of classification by no means characterizes this new generation.

The justification for the use of the year 1938, similar to that of Spain's well-established Generation of 1898, is based as much on political-social foment as upon literary innovation.

The single most influential event outside Chile was the bloody Spanish Civil War. Commencing in 1936, by 1938 the war still maintained its crushing effect upon the minds of many Chileans who saw their spiritual mother killing her own offspring. Fear spread among many Latin Americans, a fear of the fall of their own country into the barbarisms of civil conflict. The war became a grim and vital reality to the people, rather than a distant conflict to be read about and forgotten. The artists of the generation of 1938 were torn by the civil war as children of quarreling parents. They viewed it as a manifestation of violence in a world which was dividing herself into two camps—Nazis/Fascists against the powers of democracy. In 1938 it was only an ideological, word war; in 1939 and 1941 its violence burst upon a shocked world. Arturo Torres-Rioseco observed that: "Since 1940 European and North American influences have transformed the Chilean novel. Marxism has entered unrestrained in literature and none of the novelists who began to write around 1938 escaped its power. Violence, rebellion, and candid Messianism again appear in the novels of this period."[20]

After many years of absence, Pablo Neruda returned to Chile in 1937, with *Spain in My Heart*. He, too, felt the pain and anguish of war's destruction and a need for rebuilding. "Behold my lifeless house, Behold my broken Spain," echoed the sentiments of millions of Latin Americans. The second edition was published in Chile in 1938, with eighteen frightening photographs. The book was a poetic, but concrete, embodiment of the fears his countrymen suffered during the Spanish Civil War.

Neruda created the "Alliance of Chilean Intellectuals in Defense of Culture," in November, 1937, providing a unifying force among the country's artists, who often gathered in the Amaya Bar to discuss the literary goings-on. The magazine *Aurora de Chile* was conceived and published, with Neruda as director. In this publication Juan Godoy wrote the manifesto, "Angurrientismo y cultura" ("Satiety and Culture"), for his followers. These intellectuals held great love for the *roto*, the hardened common man, and often went in pilgrimage to the Square of the *Roto* in Santiago. Another periodical, *Multitud*, was begun in 1938. The subtitle clearly expresses the seemingly contradictory goals of both the magazine and the generation of 1938: "Magazine of the People and High Society." Godoy's "Satiety and Culture" also appeared in this publication. More decidedly political in nature than *Aurora de Chile*, *Multitud* became the mouthpiece of the Popular Front. It fulfilled a vital unifying function, bringing together art and politics. The magazine was published, sporadically, under the direction of poet Pablo de Rokha.

Other cultural developments speeded the emergence of a new literary movement: expansion and creation of literary supplements to many Chilean newspapers; Manuel Rojas' essays, *From Poetry to Revolution*, in 1938; the traveling theater company of Margarita Xirgú representing García Lorca's poetic tragedies. Perhaps most significant was the daily contact of the intellectuals in the Pedagogical Institute of the University of Chile. In this atmosphere a new rebellious generation took on the burden of superseding the masterworks of earlier Chilean literature.

II *Literary Influences on the Generation*

Attempting to define generational influences, the artists of 1938 have freely discussed their inspiration. Fernando Alegría, novelist turned critic, has been especially expansive.[21] From the great Russian novelists, Gogol, Dostoevski, Turgenev, Gorki, the writers of 1938 accepted the mandate to turn artistic creation toward man's social responsibility, to achieve an idealistic harmony of man's spirit with the forces of nature. In short, literature was to be not only artistic but socially functional; and it could not be separated from the reality in which the writer lived. The second influencing factor listed by Alegría was the lively, enduring Chilean poetry written between 1915 and 1930. Gabriela Mistral, Vicente Huidobro, Pablo de Rokha, Carlos Pezoa Véliz, and, logically, Pablo Neruda created a rich heritage and exercised multiple influences in Chile. Purity of creation, a subtle localism, discovery of the eternal aspects of the masses, preoccupation with language and style, the spiritual dimension of landscape, and the lyricism of the country and its people were direct influences from Chile's renowned poets and were incorporated into the prose and poetry of the new literary movement.

Another outspoken member of the generation, Volodia Teitelboim, in writing of his contemporaries, states that many in the
group began as poets but, finding the masses unreceptive, turned
to the novel. In particular, the "discovery" of three now-classic
Latin American novels turned them to prose. These were: *La
vorágine* (*The Vortex*), *Don Segundo Sombra,* and *El Señor
Presidente* (*Mr. President*).[22] *Mr. President* was not published
until 1946, but its techniques and author were known in Chile.
The writer, Miguel Angel Asturias, received the Nobel Prize
for Literature in 1967. Logically, scores of other novels and short
stories influenced individual members of Chile's generation of
1938, but the three mentioned above were known, read, and
reread by nearly all of the ambitious young writers. These works
incorporated certain characteristics the generation considered
worthy of emulation—in particular, their harmonious union of
prose and poetry. Though each dealt with nationalistic themes
or legends, they seemed to vibrate a chord of universality, common to all Latin America. Such was the challenge facing the
new generation—to re-create the particular, distinctive realities
of Chile without sacrificing the universal values of lasting
literature.

Juan Godoy, in *Sangre de murciélago,* gives the most complete breakdown of the artists who influenced his generation,
including not only writers, but painters, musicians, and sculptors. In politics, Marx and Lenin were the idols. In literature
the influences were multiple: the Russian novelists Gogol, Gon-
charov, Dostoevski, Chekhov, Gorki, and especially Andreyev,
with his "Lazarus" and "The Red Laugh." From France, Proust,
Valéry, and Gide; Baudelaire, Nerval, and Rimbaud. Poe and
Walt Whitman, "the tumultuous North American," were widely
read and quoted in Chile. From Spanish tradition it was the Mod-
ernists Darío and Herrera y Reissig, and from the Generation
of 1898, Unamuno, Ortega, Azorín, Baroja, and Antonio Machado,
who lived in the minds and on the lips of Godoy and his contemporaries. Rodin in sculpture; Goya, Cézanne, Gauguin, Van
Gogh, Matisse, and Picasso in painting; Nietzsche, Bergson, Hus-
serl, Dilthey, and Kierkegaard in philosophy; Moussorgsky,
Debussy, Bach, Falla, and Albéniz in music.[23] This imposing
list shows the wide range of culture which served as a base
for the generation of 1938, a group of writers who felt obligated

to read widely, absorb all possible influence, and bring culture and universality to Chilean letters.

In summary, six major influences bore directly on the generation: (1) The great Russian novelists of the late nineteenth and early twentieth centuries; (2) Chilean poetry from 1915 to 1935; (3) three poetic novels often categorized as "super-regionalistic," completed in 1924, 1925, and 1926 (*The Vortex, Mr. President*, and *Don Segundo Sombra*, respectively); (4) the "Generation of 1898" in Spanish letters; (5) late nineteenth- and early twentieth-century philosophers who stressed man's irrationality and temporal anguish; and (6) a synesthetic smattering of painters, musicians, and sculptors. It is obvious from this brief study of literary antecedents that the new writers wanted to move Chilean letters into the main currents of world literature; they felt that they had talents to compete with the best. At the same time, however, it is readily seen that their inspiration came from writers of previous decades and even the previous century. They found little in the early 1930's, save Chilean poetry, worthy of emulation. Even the Latin American novels that most nearly touched them were produced in the 1920's. Like many new literary movements, the young writers found little use for the regionalistic, realistic prose produced during the previous twenty years in Chile. They had broader, more optimistic plans—to penetrate the soul of Chile and find the hidden, universal values in her life and literature.

III   *The Objectives of a New Generation*

Shaped by influences from world literature and by the political events of their own country, a young group of writers, almost unnoticed at first, began to form its credo. They had a mission to fulfill, and many felt the need to materialize their goals in writing. First the writers themselves, Miguel Serrano, Carlos Droguett, Juan Godoy, Nicomedes Guzmán and later the critics, Ricardo A. Latcham, Francisco Santana, Volodia Teitelboim, defined and identified goals. Some critics have explained the objectives of the generation of 1938 as being simply anti-Criollist. Whatever the Criollists did, the new promotion reversed, echoed the critics. This oversimplification is unsound for two basic reasons. First, the new artists had a series of concepts and objectives of their own, independent of Criollism and based on influences of Latin American and European literature.

Second, and more personal: most of the participants in the new literature were students or friends of Mariano Latorre. They respected his ideas and recognized his genius. They found many lasting values in his works and, rather than completely destroy, they desired only to go deeper, to more thoroughly penetrate the life of man. Juan Godoy maintains that his generation expressed positive and not negative values; it sought to live in harmony with its predecessors. He sees this quality as a literary virtue. Criollism for Juan Godoy was merely a springboard. According to one reviewer, Godoy creates "A literature of man agitating nature; not a literature where nature has deformed an assassinated man."[24]

The first objective, then, might be described as a departure from, but not a rejection of, the Criollist school of the previous generation. In specifics:

(1) Criollism had dealt mainly with the *external aspects* of man—his appearance, his speech, his actions. The new generation accepted these human characteristics as necessary, but sensed a need to get to the *internal problems*—thoughts, decisions, anguish, fear. These "internals" reflect the eternal, the poetic, the universal qualities of man in the contemporary world. If properly explored and dramatized they would lift Chilean literature to international status.

(2) In Criollism, *language* recorded, much like a camera, the exact speech of the country peasant, with all its deformations and oddities. The new movement saw language as a complex symbol system for painting word images—a basis for stylistic innovation as well as for a description of reality.

(3) *Novelistic action,* for most Criollists, was episodic and moved in orderliness from one scene to the next. The generation of 1938 added techniques of circular action, imagined action in the mind of the protagonist, and generally broke up the system of episodic progression in the narrative.

(4) *Man,* often a product of naturalistic determination, was fixed in time and space. On Panta and Domingo Persona, traditional Criollist characters in Latorre, however astute and endearing, are always On Panta and Domingo Persona—nothing more. Godoy and his peers, on the other hand, saw man as more than a stationary unit; they viewed him through a series of symbols, dramatically linked to the past but capable of participating in future eternities. Man was no longer seen as

one-dimensional, but as a complex soul, with the capacity to
be and become many things.

A second major goal of the generation was to make literature
socially functional. The author was not to remain neutral to
problems confronting his country and humanity in general but
was to enter into a campaign to elucidate and solve. In 1938,
with the victory of the Popular Front, it became a near obsession to give literary category to the struggles for economic
emancipation of the working class. Political victory stimulated
artistic activity. Where Criollism had dedicated extensive sections to describing man's relationship to nature, the writers
of 1938 were more interested in dramatizing the relationship of
one man to another in a social aggregate. This literary concern
for man's relationship to his fellow man has been described as
"Sociological Realism," and Juan Godoy is acknowledged as
one of its founders in Chile.[25]

Godoy takes pride in creating characters who rebel to better
their social condition, making life a struggle against established
injustices. The writer functions to clarify and show possible
solutions to these injustices. The objective, writes one critic,
"is the desire to see an improvement in the lot of the *huaso*, the
roto, and in general all underprivileged men; they wish to see
him emerge as a respected individual possessing dignity and
integrated into his rightful place in Chilean society."[26]

A third objective of the generation is that of characterizing
Chile and Chileans in relation to the whole of the contemporary
world.[27] This characterization goes beyond the local concern
for Chile to a concern for all Latin America. Two phases may
be seen. The first is the more localistic view, dealing with Chile,
and a desire to penetrate not only the land but the soul that
lies beneath—to discover what is truly Chilean. The search penetrates geographical and psychological regions as yet unexplored
in Chilean literature. Francisco Coloane depicts southern Chile,
Punta Arenas to Tierra del Fuego, in his *Cabo de Hornos* (*Cape
Horn*). Miguel Serrano "hears a call from the icefields of Antarc-
tica." Nicomedes Guzmán's "light comes from the sea." There
are novels and short stories of the "Great North," the "Lesser
North," the Central Valley, the mountains, Chiloé, Magallanes
Province, and so on. It becomes the writer's duty to explore
every corner of his country. The setting for Juan Godoy's first
novel is neither the city nor the country but the hovel outskirts

of Santiago. In such areas, often ignored by previous writers, the generation of 1938 unveiled new realities, aiding in the definition of Chile's essence. In this virgin literary clime, the second phase of the goal is accomplished: the discovery and exposition of the human soul in touch with ebullient life. These principles extend the movement far beyond mere regionalistic concepts into more universal realms. When completely understood, the problems of man in Chile do not differ from those of man in Mexico or Russia, the writers felt. The study of man—integral and internal, as a social being—was to become the most prominent objective of the young generation, and would universalize Chilean literature.

The Criollists of the previous generation had completed only a part of the first phase of this two-pronged objective; they had depicted character types in scattered regions of Chile. The new generation would discover all of Chile while revealing the universal characteristics that unite Chileans with the rest of the world—the aspirations, tragedies, sufferings of man. Their writings were not to be just another mode of expression in Chilean literature but the expression of a people, of an entire continent.

The desire to portray the realistic essence of Chile and capture the universal qualities of man's spirit led to the fourth objective of the generation, but it also brought complex problems. To return to the photographic, tape-recorder realism of the Criollists would stifle universality. To ignore the realities of Chilean life, writing of a world with no national roots could achieve universality, but would fail to depict the soul of Chile. Godoy's *Angurrientos* reconciles these opposing poles by a "constant balance between realistic everyday elements and a free expression loosed from the ordinary, *almost poetic. . . .* This poetry reflects a reality and also a temperament, reconciling loyalty to objectivity with fidelity to subjectivity."[28] Poetry, or the use of poetic devices in prose, was to become the vehicle for elevating the new literature to more meaningful universal levels. The reader notes the visible influence of Chilean poetry on the new writers: more abundant metaphors, poetic fragility, rhythm in prose and mythical association. That poetic prose style was a definite objective of the young authors is further evidenced by the Latin American novels in which they found inspiration: *Don Segundo Sombra, The Vortex,* and *Mr. Presi-*

dent. These novels showed that poetic style could achieve local-istic expression, yet still touch the problems encountered by every man. Further, they taught that man could be linked with myth to further ennoble him and give him stature. Don Segundo, for example; is seen as "a phantom, a shadow, something that passes quickly and is more of an idea than a being, something that attracted me with the strength of a calm pool whose depths suck in the current of the river." Thus, in many novels of the new generation, man is linked with some figure from Greek myth-ology, with a folkloric myth, or with a particular feeling or attitude. In this fashion, the life of one individual transcends the time and space of twentieth-century Chile and may bring the sought-after universal poetic which the generation desired.

The four objectives mentioned above—superseding the Criol-list school, social involvement of literature, penetration into the Chilean and continental soul, and a more poetic prose—never appeared in any one written document, nor were they agreed upon by prior arrangement. They were often tossed about orally but were never written down nor formally accepted as a credo. They are this writer's observations, viewing the gen-eration in retrospect. Many other aims could be listed, especially if one studies the works of a single author. The above list serves as a framework in which the generation, initially at least, set out to raise its country's literature from Criollist to universal.

The generation of 1938 did not maintain unity over a given period, fighting valiantly for its cause, only to succumb to a younger, more energetic generation. On the contrary, it split into various factions and within fifteen years seemed to dissipate itself. The year 1938 was the jumping-off point, when several strong figures of the new group won disciples to their causes. Godoy's Neo-Realism (Angurrientism) was the most vigorous and largest part of the generation. Surrealism attracted many authors and experienced a brief but vital manifestation in the prose of Miguel Serraño and the poetry of the Mandrágora group. Some Chileans include María Luisa Bombal as a separate facet in the generation, by virtue of her age and the dates of her first publications.[29] The heterogeneous nature of the genera-tion set the stage for several dramatic polemics among writers of the same age. Different from other new literary generations who have verbally struggled with the older regime, the members of 1938 themselves formed into several different camps, warring against each other rather than attacking the old generals. Various anthologies appeared in 1938, 1941, 1945, and 1949, some claiming to be the "true" anthology of the generation, all vying for preeminence. By the early 1950's the generation had spent itself.

The branch denominated Neo-Realist (or, Sociological Realism) was by far the most widely read and criticized arm of the generation. As recognized leader of this group, Juan Godoy christened the new child with his own term, "Angurrientism."

IV *Angurrientism*

Two factors facilitated the formation of a literary group centered around Godoy. First was the personal magnetism of this student officer in the Pedagogical Institute. His vociferous leadership in literary discussions made him the unofficial but unchallenged leader. The second factor, more concrete, is the appearance in 1939 of two magazine articles outlining cultural values and literary concepts for the new movement. Authored by Godoy, they set forth specific objectives for the generation in relation to previous Chilean literature.

Godoy's "Breve ensayo sobre el roto" ("Short Essay on the Toughened Laborer") appeared in the January, 1939 issue of *Atenea*. Mariano Latorre added a lengthy editor's note to the first page, explaining that the author, Juan Godoy, was the creator of a new literary promotion, Angurrientism. Latorre saw Angurrientism as a Neo-Criollist movement, differing from his own Criollism only in its psychological penetration of man.

Godoy's thesis is that, to comprehend Chilean life and culture and Chile's contribution to universal culture, it is necessary to fully understand the *roto*. (The word means broken or ragged and applies to a poor, but proud, tough workingman, an ambiguous character type associated with poverty-stricken sections in Chilean urban centers. He fits well into the concept of *Machismo* but is proudly independent and unique to Chile.) The *roto*, not the *huaso* (the dynamic, boisterous country rustic), reveals the true nature of Chile, argues Godoy. Godoy is careful not to directly challenge Latorre's popularity but clearly denies the value in superficially depicting the life of the peasant. To insure that his readers know who and what the *roto* is, Godoy mentions several characteristics: he is a Chilean, usually poor, endowed with an exaggerated individualism and excessive self-confidence;

he is a virile, nonmethodical wandering soul who lives only for
the moment—eating, drinking, loving, and even dying in excess.
The most fitting description of the type, however, is his Angurrientism. Godoy defines the term, apparently used here for the
first time in literature, as simply "an excess of life," too much
life; "The *roto* leaves nothing on the plate of life; he eats everything up in a single day" (34). The Angurrientism concept
explains the nature of the *roto,* and thus of Chile, for to Godoy
the common man is Chile. While the country peasant exists only
in a limited geographical and temporal sphere, the hardened
commoner, says Godoy, typifies all of Chile in all time. This
universal, timeless quality appealed greatly to the body of
idealistic young writers.

Godoy condemns Joaquín Edwards Bello's novel, *El roto*
(1920), as a blasphemy against the Chilean people, lacking in
empathy for the tragic figure it develops. But in certain lyric
poets, such as Carlos Pezoa Véliz and Neruda of *Residence on
Earth—2,* the spirit of the *roto* begins to appear.[30] Now it be-
hooves the younger generation of prose writers to immortalize
the *roto,* "the only hero type in Chile" (38).

The essay ends on a pessimistic note, revealing a characteristic trait of Angurrientism. Godoy writes that common men
"Are masters of themselves. Masters of nothing" (40). It is precisely from this negative point that Godoy wishes to commence. Though the *roto* has nothing in a material sense, he
reveals a richness of soul, a store of untapped wealth within.
Angurrientism would tap and refine this wealth for the literary
world.

The overtones exuding from the article are biting condemnations of previous Chilean society and politics, based on wealth
and exploitation, which had attempted to destroy the unique
individuality of the commoner. Godoy's attempts to seek out
the masses as the source of real values in society and to deal with
man as a social being indicate the political concern traceable
to the victory of the Popular Front in 1938. Social orientation
would now prevail in literature. The objectives of the new
movement, however, were not purely social, they were still
strongly literary. Godoy declared the necessity of three ideals:
(1) to penetrate the soul of the *roto,* (2) to know his folklore,
and (3) to destroy his imposed inferiority complex (37).

A second, more encompassing essay saw light eight months

later, in *Aurora de Chile,* a semiofficial organ of the young writers. Entitled "Angurrientismo y cultura" ("Satiety and Culture"), it gives the background as well as the ideology for the movement.

In an editor's note at the foot of the first page, probably added by Godoy, sixteen authors and their Angurrientist works are listed. Together with recent novels and short stories, Godoy includes poems of Claudio Indo, Víctor Franzani, an essay by Jorge Millas, the music of Moisés Miranda and Carmen Godoy, and the ceramic works of Ramón Miranda. This curious collection of artists is indicative of a movement bent on including all forms of Chilean cultural expression, rather than literature alone.

The definition Godoy presented in the article became the classic, often-repeated watchwords of his generation: *"Angurrientos* is above all, a movement of intuition of Chilean Cultural essence, a VITAL DESIRE FOR LIFE! It examines the natural soul which has engraved its values on this land. . . . To closely examine dynamic Angurrientist concepts is, therefore, to demonstrate the essence of Chile in her vital development, the sum of an insurgent soul that fulfills her culture and destiny."[31]

In typical Marxist terminology, he argues that the heroic figure of all class struggles, the formidable archetype, has always been the *roto.* He postulates that to find the soul of the continent, a study of the past is unnecessary; the real essence can be seen in the great collective human archetypes. "The proletariat and worker of Hispanic America are the concrete expression. The Mexican Pelao, the Peruvian Cholo, the Chilean Roto, the Argentine Gaucho, the Venezuelan Llanero, the Ecuadorian Montuvio, etc. These are the heroes of Hispanic-American unity and culture. . . . In this fashion we view the personality of our masses and their divergent cultural contributions enriching the Unity of Man as he confronts the Universe" (4). Although not a new theory,[32] the universal nature of the *roto* was the one aspect which gave a seemingly continental flavor to Angurrientism. The artists of the generation felt they were being strongly nationalistic, yet quite universal. Whether this is altogether possible may be debated, but it was an honest attempt to get Chilean literature out of the narrow limits of nationalistic movements.

Godoy sees Angurrientism as a broad, unlimited movement, dealing with the relationship of man to the universe. Man is

the center of the movement. Godoy affirms that his is a movement based on reality, not a geographically limited reality but
the reality of man's soul. He recognizes that it is only a beginning for deeper realizations and concludes the essay tersely:
"Let us write ravagingly."

Running continuously through the essay like a leitmotif in
music are three expressions which have come to be representative of the movement: (1) "Vital desire for life," (2) "Transition
from the commonplace to the universal," and (3) "A movement
of intuition of Chilean cultural essence." Each of these phrases
help to define Angurrientism, but all three are necessary to avoid
a distorted view of the new literary ideals. Even in Chile the
concept was not fully understood by the general public and
was often misconstrued by critics.

The first phase of the above definition is the least understood.
Coined by Ortega, it was common in the period. "Vital desire
for life," as used by Godoy, has two distinct meanings. First,
it refers to subject matter and the created characters in literature. In his voracious appetite for life, the *angurriento* lives
each moment to its fullest. There is no passivity; life is action;
not even crumbs are left on the plate of life.

The second meaning refers to the author's hunger or desire
to perfect his own style. To write good Angurrientist literature,
a novelist must not be content merely to reproduce reality as a
camera or tape recorder might do; he has to concern himself
with a personal style and take care *how* he is getting across to
the reader as well as *what* he is saying.

"Transition from the commonplace to the universal" deals
with the concept of giving a base, broader than pure
nationalism, to the new literature. While it must characterize
a true Chilean type, the *roto*, it must also link this type to other
national literary prototypes to achieve some degree of universality or cosmic relationship. The chief theme of this literature
will be man and his solitude. Language will of necessity be
nationalistic, but the problems dealt with will be those of every
man everywhere. It is important to comprehend this desire to
depict a cosmos larger than national borders, since critics, almost
without exception, have viewed Angurrientism as purely Chilean,
with no extranational significance. Critics have dealt only with
the interesting, but superficial, levels of language and Chilean
folklore, without examining universal relationships.

The third phase, "A movement of intuition of Chilean cultural essence," succinctly expresses the major goal of the developing generation of 1938. Its rare grammatical construction is an example of the first principle of Angurrientism: stylistic deviation from tradition. The significant concept in the phrase is that Angurrientism is to be not so much a descriptive as an intuitive penetration into Chile's heart. Only feelings, thoughts, and mental attitudes can express the soul of the *roto*, and not mechanical description of landscape or imitation of speech. By intuition on the part of the creator the true characteristics of a Chilean can be displayed.

The term "Angurrientism," as applied to a literary movement, was the invention of Juan Godoy. In mid-1938 he finished the novel *Angurrientos,* and its enthusiastic reception among friends made it a natural as a title for the new school. In fact, it appears that even before the completion of the novel, Godoy had coined the new word to explain his own and his contemporaries' objectives. Martín Alonso asserts that *angurriento,* an Americanism, comes from the word *angurria,* used since the seventeenth century to signify egotism and a desire to eat or win. The adjective *angurrientos,* or its synonym, *angurrioso,* indicates a starved or hungry person who wants to eat everything at one sitting.[33] It was upon this connotation that Godoy based the new literary movement. Various definitions for the trend, usually based on Godoy's *Angurrientos,* have been proffered. Víctor Valezuela calls the movement a "school of pessimism."[34] Although the novel has never appeared in English, the title *Angurrientos* has appeared translated as *Gluttons*[35] and as *The Insatiable Ones.*[36] Both translations aptly describe the idea, although gluttons could easily be misconstrued as referring chiefly to food, which is not a correct interpretation of the novel's theme. Many critics have stated that the term applies only to physical hunger,[37] but others have caught the vision of something more inclusive: "insatiables, eversearching, or, in a word, human beings who walk within themselves, seeking the truth of their own attitudes from inside."[38] According to Godoy himself, Angurrientism is: "Starving humanity, reaching for the spiritual, all-embracing unity of mankind."[39] Godoy uses physical hunger to reflect a state of dissatisfaction with life, a spiritual search for improvement, and an all-embracing concern for humanity. The Chilean *roto* was the ideal subject for this new literature. The duty of

the writers in the group was to treat these problems with new
techniques and depth of style. They viewed Chilean reality as
multiple, and hence diverse techniques and styles, were not
only permissible but desirous and necessary.

A group of thirty to forty writers associated with and formed
around Godoy in 1938. The initiator of this group recalls the
following as belonging to the movement:[40]

Fernando Alegría	Manuel Guerrero
Guillernmo Atías	Nicomedes Guzmán
Abelardo Barahona	Claudio Indo
Pedro de la Barra	Jorge Jobet
Daniel Belmar	Reinaldo Lomboy
Baltazar Castro	Alfredo Llana
Oscar Castro	Luis Merino Reyes
Francisco Coloane	Juan Modesto Castro
Carlos Droguett	Raul Morález Alvárez
Víctor Franzani	Edmundo de la Parra
Juan Godoy	Nicasio Tangol
Luis González Zenteno	Volodia Teitelboim
Leoncio Guerrero	Carlos Vattier

Parra and Vattier were essentially short-story writers: Franzani, Indo, and Jobet were the poets. Belmar and Modesto Castro were slightly older than the other members of the movement
but identified with the newly declared ideals. From this group
came novels, plays, short stories, and poetry in the Angurrientist
vein. Alegría's initial prose, *Recabarren* and *Consejas del gran
río* (*Tales of the Great River*) are deeply colored with Angurrientism. *Témpano vivo* (*The Living Iceberg*) by Coloane,
Parra's *Consejas de un río vivo* (*Tales of a Living River*), and
L. Guerrero's *Pichamán* are collections of short stories in line
with the "Vital desire for life." Franzani's *Arquitectura de la
sombra* (*The Architecture of Shadow*) and *Un hombre apunta
a su imagen* (*Man Aims at Himself*) by Indo exemplify Angurrentism in poetry. Pedro de la Barra's *La feria* (*Marketplace*)
brings similar ideas to Chilean drama. But it is in the medium
of the novel that the movement experiences its apogee. Lomboy's
Ranquil, Guzmán's *Los hombres oscuros* (*Men of Darkness*),
and, of course, *Angurrientos* are three convincing examples of the
forceful prose of the new generation. Nearly all the members of
the school tried their hand at this form and produced scores of

novels, many now forgotten or unpublished, but all embodying the techniques and themes of Angurrientism.

The autonomous group of Angurrientist writers maintained a unity for approximately five years, gathering around Juan Godoy in 1938, but assuming separate styles and themes by 1942 and 1943. Some novelists continued for a decade or more, but by 1943 the group had lost its autonomy. Juan Godoy sees no rejection of his values and ideas in this dispersion; he has stated: "An idea was launched and exploration continued; afterwards each seaman went his separate way."[41] As the group began to break up, the members maintained the guidelines set by Angurrientism. "The Angurrientist writers of 1938, even though scattered at present, nevertheless seem to recall the direction outlined by Juan Godoy."[42] Many used the prescribed themes and adapted them to stylistic nuances. Godoy considers Alegría's *Caballo de copas* (*My Horse González*), 1957, for example, as an Angurrientist work. Godoy himself undertook new themes in later novels, but he never lost the frenetic, imagistic style that dominated *Angurrientos*.

While Godoy applied the term "Angurrientism" to what many assume to be a purely Chilean movement, the precepts of the several writers coincide almost exactly with the broader, more universal Neo-Realist movement in world literature. If the Realism of the nineteenth century was to be an objective, representative view of man, its return in the twentieth hoped to add even further dimensions to the real world created in literature. Guillermo de Torre has studied Neo-Realism in Italy and finds it to be a reaction against the highly imaginative, artistic works of D'Annunzio and a return to observable reality as the basis for literary inspiration.[43] While de Torre limits himself to the movement in only one area, the principles of Neo-Realism extended to the literatures, art, and even film-making of many countries. An examination of the general characteristics of Neo-Realism will demonstrate its similarities to Godoy's prose and establish a link with Chilean Angurrientism.

The protagonists of Neo-Realist prose generally proceed from the lower class and represent the values of that sector of society.[44] The novel abandons myth and fantasy in favor of a return to the immediate and daily happenings of life. But instead of presenting life in rigid temporal continuum (as so often occurred in earlier Realistic fiction), the author creates a disconnected universe in

both time and space. Reality is viewed on a multiplicity of levels
—psychological, spiritual, symbolic, surrealistic, as well as
visual. The great ambition of Neo-Realistic writers, as defined
by the Marxist critic György Lukacs, is to portray "the total
man." The frequent use of the spoken language of the lower
class and the emphasis on the problems of man relating, or
most often not relating, to his work and surroundings purports
to fulfill this ambition. Within the poverty segment the author
finds wealth of internal riches, men who naturally exude the
only authentic characteristics of their nation. "The ambition of
these authors is to reflect the true face of a country, of a people,
and to gather the most sincere and antirhetorical examination
of a nation's conscience."[45] Only in the presentation of this
character type can the real spontaneity of life be captured in
literature: so argue these authors. Neo-Realistic novels tend to
be presentational rather than representational; that is, characters and scenes are presented directly, with much dialogue, rather
than through narrative summary.

Yet however glamorous and all-encompassing the above goals
may seem, the movement is fraught with inherent paradox. It
avoids a large sector of humanity, a segment it considers artificial and hence unworthy. As a result, it too often creates character types, representatives of a single class, rather than re-creating
human beings. The oversaturation of too much and too limited
Realism results in a deformed reality that frustrates the original
intent. The selection and recombination of life, necessary for any
great literary work, is often absent and results in the creation of
a chaotic series of unimportant details mixed with the indispensable.

In an attempt to supersede these paradoxes, Godoy filled his
own prose with many artistic and selective devices, not content
with the possible lack of transcendence he foresaw in Angurrientism if it were merely Neo-Realism in Chile. He encouraged
other writers to follow suit, but few were able to carry off the
relatively vulgar thematic material in a poetic style. Nicomedes
Guzmán, next to Godoy, most nearly approaches the goal.
Through his amazing ability with language Godoy was able to
poeticize and universalize much of the sordid baseness in which
other Neo-Realists reveled. It is this quality, the poetization of
a previously forbidding reality, that shocks the uninitiated reader
and that elevates Godoy to the position of a first-rate prose

writer. One critic, Adolf Ramírez, finds difficulty in even fitting Godoy into his thesis on "The Chilean Novel of Social Protest" due to Godoy's emphasis on artistic and folkloric expression instead of on pure social exposition. "There is evidence in Godoy's *Angurrientos* that beautiful effects can sometimes be obtained even with repulsive subjects.... The incident ["Herminia's Revenge"] in itself is not appetizing. But it becomes beautiful and deeply affecting, for the author describes with tragic force the misery of these wretched starving people."[46] Godoy's Angurrentism sprouts from his extraordinary abilities to adapt Neo-Realistic themes to his own imaginative style, a unique creation in Chilean and world literature.

"A literary generation is better seen by its descendants than by its participants"[47] has often been the sentiment of critics as well as of writers. Temporal or physical proximity often distorts vision and evaluation. Even though many of the authors of the generation of 1938 are still writing, sufficient time has elapsed that critical judgments can now validly assess contributions and directions.

In Chile, where new literary generations seem to crop up at short inervals (every ten years, according to Latcham in *La Nación,* August 24, 1959), prose writers of the 1938 movement have given ground to the newer generation of 1950, headed by Enrique Lafourcade, José Donoso, and José Manuel Vergara. It is a more cosmopolitan, less nationalistic generation than the previous one. Yet Fernando Alegría feels that the two coincide in their basic nature: the desire to penetrate Chilean reality and to find its social and psychological values. Despite this similarity, however, the mere formation of a new literary generation places the older movement in a position more accessible to valid examination.

From the literature produced by the myriad writers of the generation of 1938, two major conclusions are evident. The first deals with theme; man becomes the center of the literature from 1938 on. The theme of man as a multiple being, wrestling with self and society, replaces the previous Criollist literature which depicted man as a static type. Man takes on symbolic, universal aspects as he overcomes problems of fear, loneliness, and social subjugation. There is a more thorough delving into the mystery of existence than ever before. Man, beset with universal problems, is the unifying theme of the new literature.

The second conclusion, especially as it concerns Godoy, deals with style, where a newly found poetic intensity lends universality and enhances the created world. Following examples of the best Latin American novels and the best writers in recent world literature—Joyce, Proust, Huxley, Faulkner—the generation of 1938 consciously brought innovation of style and technique to Chilean letters. Literature based on symbols and metaphor, instead of realistic description, took control of the new writers. Poetic narration intensified the works of the generation. Man as the center of Godoy's created world and the style and narrative technique of his novels will be the major studies of the following chapters, following a brief overview of the author's prose production.

CHAPTER 2

Literary Trajectory

B EFORE examining the separate artistic elements of Godoy's works it is necessary to view the novels in their totality and detail their narrative action. Only after the prose is understood on this basic level can the study of style and technique of poetic Neo-Realism be justified.

Godoy's first published novel *Angurrientos,* appeared in 1940; his last work, *El impedido,* was completed in 1968. Thus, over a period of nearly thirty years the author has been active in literary creation and still hopes to complete projected novels. While *Angurrientos* is still his best known novel, it is only one of four; the others are: *La cifra solitaria* (1945), *Sangre de murciélago* (1959), and *El impedido* (1968). *El gato de la maestranza* (1952) is the only published volume of short stories and contains five short creations: "El gato de la maestranza" ("Cat in the Roundhouse"), "El profesor y unos pelusas" ("The Professor and the Young Rowdies"), "El ramal o el canario bombero" ("The Whip, or the Spouting Canary"), "Un inspector de sanidad" ("A Public Health Inspector"), and "La venganza de Herminia" ("Herminia's Revenge"). The last story was an intercalated chapter from *Angurrientos* and used here to more fully complete the collection. "Un inspector de sanidad" had previously appeared in separate publication by the National School of Graphic Arts, in 1950. One final short story, "Sombras" ("Shadows"), reached the public in 1966 through the Chilean magazine *Mapocho.* Four novels and six short stories constitute the author's entire literary production.

I Angurrientos

Angurrientos (*The Insatiable Ones*), the first and best known among Godoy's works, is a 250-page seemingly disordered novel par excellence of the Chilean *roto.* The seeming disorder is true disorder if one judges the novel from the standpoint of traditional novels of realistic bent. Godoy has knowingly and intentionally introduced this disorder in a somewhat Joycean attempt to grasp an elusive reality that in itself is tumultuous and confused. The reader is made aware of the ancient literary conflict between structure and theme; Godoy chooses to view a disordered society by means of a disarranged technique. At least four areas, to be discussed in detail in later chapters, demonstrate this technique of disorder: temporal, spatial, structural, and character relationships. No less than forty characters, more if minor nameless figures are reckoned, parade before the reader. Their identification is made doubly difficult by the fact that many are mere character types, supposedly typical *rotos*, and never achieve any degree of autonomy. Structural order is challenged by the inclusion of popular verses, the words to folk dances, and the intercalation of six separate short narratives which serve to expand but not to advance the action. Similarly, time and space are segmented and superimposed, causing the reader to create for himself the artificial order necessary for comprehension but not essential for the feeling and emotional experience intended by the creator.

The scattered events of *Angurrientos* unite around the central protagonist, Edmundo, a young Socialist enjoying the advantages of being educated in a university and imbued with the mission of instilling social consciousness in his countrymen. Experiencing the bitter realities of alcohol, sex, and the meaningless life of the *roto*, he hopelessly lays down his mission and sadly conforms to an amorphous future as the novel terminates. Edmundo "had tried to get the drunkards out of their stupid existence as beasts of burden, inciting rebellion in them, showing them their rights, dragging them into the fight" (47). But they did not respond, and Edmundo drops into the defeat of alcohol as do the majority of the other characters in the novel; unable to change himself, he follows the futility of others. Obviously, the message is not a positive one: man appears to be thwarted in both personal improvement and social betterment. Edmundo's self-defeat symbolizes the plight of the nation, if the *roto* is to be taken as an authentic national representative, as Godoy postulates.

Edmundo does not preach communism or any one type of socialism but follows Godoy's own philosophy (and that of the liberal political APRISTA movement in Peru) that each country must work out its own problems in accord with tradition, situation, and possibility. In reality, as previously implied, Godoy is not pounding out a hard social message, nor is he attacking government or foreign intervention. He is merely depicting a human type in an oppressed environment and views individual change as requisite to societal advancement.

While Edmundo is the one major continuous character in the novel, his interaction with the Ovalle family is fundamental to understanding. The opening scene transpires in the dirty, oppressive atmosphere of the Ovalle shack where adolescent Eulogio and his sensuous sister Wanda live with their parents, the once immoral Mercedes and the red-haired, tough Pedro (often mentioned as Sargento Ovalle). Typical of the literary image of the toughened lower class, Pedro does not work in any permanent job but merely exists for, by, and with his fighting cocks. The narrative action of the novel follows this family, frequently returning to their hovel-home near the cemetery and next door to a cheap bar, to portray the filth and futility of existence. Edmundo relates to the family through his budding love for Wanda. Pedro Ovalle, a Protestant, although warm and endearing to the reader, maintains the family in squalid poverty, betting, winning, and usually losing on his roosters. Cockfighting becomes the central motif of the novel; the inclusion of most of the minor figures (Augusto, Don Amaranto, and Fraile Horacio) is justified only by their involvement with Ovalle in the cockfights. Two of the intercalated stories, "Riñas de gallos" ("Cockfights") (61-82), and "El roto en el cenizo" ("The *roto* in the Ash-Colored Cock") (171-76), further expand the motif. Of particular note is the latter in which a *roto*, humiliated by the beating Chilean roosters are suffering from foreign cocks, transforms himself pantheistically into a giant rooster and easily prevails over all comers. The story need not be judged on its verisimilitude; narrated by Pedro Ovalle, it functions to affirm national values, glorify the manliness of the *roto*, and reproduce the mythical, anything-is-possible world of its narrator. Cockfighting, in excess, is one of the numerous vices of the *angurriento*. One of the few rays of hope in the novel occurs when Wanda, anguished by the prospect of a vain future, joyously and sensuously kills the best fighting cock in the house. Although she knows of her father's impending wrath she has acted and destroyed, at least symbolically, one of the causes of her distress.

Two other ravenous excesses appear as literary motifs: alcohol and sex. If the secondary characters are not involved in cock-fighting, they appear in cheap neighborhood bars, drinking the wine of forgetfulness. All view alcohol as an escape from the impossible present and none is able to drink in moderation, a further manifestation of the *roto's* natural overindulgence. Sex, too, is uncontrolled, physical, and empty. In the chapter entitled "Una vaca me mira" ("A Cow Observes Me"), Edmundo and two young drinking buddies decide to rape a passing girl but end up fighting violently among themselves over who shall be first, a matter of *roto* pride, a pride in the absurd. After the brutal scene, one of the friends, Nico, decides he is in love and, in complete abandon, flees with his future bride. Augusto, the neighborhood's best breeder of cocks, tells of a childhood sexual experience with big Berta. Two priests enjoy both real and vicarious sex experiences: physically with a wealthy old lady and symbolically as they gulp down slimy raw oysters in the chapter "Angurriosa metáfora sexual" ("A Ravenous Sexual Metaphor").

The passing of time in this novel is almost imperceptible due to the lack of third-person summary and extra comment by the narrator. The action accurs, like life, in a jumbled present, at times intense, at times hollow. No one narrator dominates, and hence the perspective gained through point of view is multiple and uneven. Past events are recalled as if they were present, as indeed they become through constant retelling and reliving. These techniques are part of an author's attempt to re-create reality as he views it rather than ordering, summarizing, and condensing. Dialogue abounds but often without full identification of speaker (as frequently occurs in man's real world). Verbal utterances and even narrative descriptions are reproduced in incomplete sentences, violating rules of grammar but following logical and experienced usage: Some sections and chapters are static and lyricize nature rather than advance plot; others are symbolic; still others are traditional narration. Based on these observations, two guidelines may be suggested to the reader of this work. First, each chapter should be read as a separate unit, not always flowing logically from the previous one. Among the twenty-five chapters some mesh well, but in the main they function as individual parts of a life puzzle. The narration follows the uneven sequence of life, an obvious effort to be realistic but expand the limits beyond the borders of the older

Realism. The second guideline is to read lyrical parts aloud, as if they were poetry. In a taped interview in 1966 Godoy read some of the poetic selections of *Angurrientos* and became completely carried away in lyric ecstasy. After concluding, in a burst of spontaneous excitement he proclaimed: "And who would deny that I'm the best poet in Chile?"[1] Although the statement need not be taken with full sincerity it does indicate that Godoy's prose fares well when read aloud and that it needs to be experienced under that condition. The unity of *Angurrientos* arises from Edmundo's quest for self and societal amelioration and from the recurrent motifs that link all lives in poverty.

II   La cifra solitaria

Even though *La cifra solitaria* (*The Lonely Cipher*) exhibits some of the aspects of the first novel (intercalation of non-progressive narrations, lyric chapters, and the like), it is much shorter and more uniform in time, place, and action. The twelve short chapters are narrated by the boy, Loncho, as he observes through a crack in the plaster the actions of his quarreling, drinking neighbors, Serafín and Chocholla. The entire novelistic action transpires in a few fatiguing hours, in one given place. The frequent spatial shifts in *Angurrientos* are gone. The action develops in a small town instead of in the outskirts of Santiago as in the previous work, and poverty in the village is somehow not as hopeless as in urban life. Loncho is filled with hope and excitement for the future; in this, he is different from the young Eulogio Ovalle or Edmundo.

Beginning his narration during a monotonous, cold rain, the boy communicates his fear of life and people (which he later outgrows), an emotion heightened when he observes drunken Serafín break the necks of several young puppies and then slash weeping Chocholla with his knife. As Loncho's mother aids the wounded lady, the rhythmic tapping of blind Golondrino draws the narrator into a new world. Either in his mind or in actual experience Loncho follows the sage old philosopher, learning that man suffers like an ox on his way to the slaughter-house. Through his associations with the mythical blind man, Loncho achieves an intellectual resignation and understanding of life. Golondrino functions as a counterpoint device, relieving

the morbidity and senseless violence that surround Loncho.
Golondrino is the only being capable of saving both the living
and the dead through his profound vision of life and his knowledge of myth and supernatural incantations.

After the interlude with the blind man, the narrator returns
to Chocholla and finds that Serafín has gone on another drinking
bout. Without showing any detail (Loncho could not because
he is spatially limited), the narrator states that Serafín has been
knifed and killed, and he is finally brought home on a stretcher.
The mythical Night of Saint John, June 24, provides a setting
of mystery and awe, as horror becomes all but a material substance for the neighbors and working friends who fear that
Satan will come at midnight to claim Serafín's belligerent soul.
The narrator hears only the sounds of the darkened death wake:
the incessant, heartbeat hammering of the coffin maker, the
uncontrolled sobbing of the women, the raucous drunkards outside, and finally the timely arrival of Golondrino's tapping.
After calmly relating various folkloric stories of oral tradition,
Golondrino is entreated to stay and save the dead man from
the wiles of the devil. Through a dramatic scene of anxiety and
terror, Golondrino repeats under pressure the "twelve magic
words" necessary to ward off Satan. The suspenseful scene
terminates as Serafín's mouth drops open producing a dead,
gurgling sound.

From the standpoint of dramatic tension, this would have
been a good unified spot to end the novel since the major
action terminated in this suspenseful scene, but Godoy's message
is not yet complete. Golondrino excuses himself from the wake
and discoursing philosophically with his dog, walks into the
rain. Seated under a fig tree during the entire night he expounds
on man and his tragic plight—a rootless existence of detachment
and fear. A complete chapter, entitled "The Lonely Cipher," is
the philosophical key to the novel. Here Godoy has aligned himself with Eduardo Mallea, Carlos Fuentes, and other contemporary novelists of Latin America who feel the powerful necessity
to explicate their philosophical ideas on life as part of the created
novelistic world.

The next morning Nacha, an adolescent (who must be compared to Edmundo of *Angurrientos* in her search for an interior
light or truth) and the narrator go to the tree and find the blind
man's dog frozen to death, arriving just in time to see Golondrino

disappearing over the mountains, into the heavens. They understand that during the night he communed with the tree and the land, found his roots, and passed away. A literal interpretation of the final scene would be that Golondrino merely died, like his dog, of freezing. Yet Godoy has given much more transcendence to the disappearance of Golondrino. He found the secret of his own life, a key for all men, and hence became as the gods, immortal, having control over creation of life and death, able to transcend fragile reality.

This ending deviates greatly from the tragic hopelessness of *Angurrientos*. It could hardly be called a realistic ending in the sense of Realism as an objective observable experience. It would seem as if Godoy had forsaken previous ideals in favor of fantasy and illusion. Yet such is not the case, for Golondrino is merely a representation of the mythical, nonrational experiences that make up the reality of the poor man in contact with the cultural, timeless roots of his society. Scoffed at by educated and supposedly reasonable classes, myth and irrational happening exist as a vital phase of the *roto's* life. "It can be seen that legend (myth) in its essence and origin is nothing more than the fantastic product of the poetry that reposes in the soul of the common man."[2] Godoy, like Borges, whose short stories deal with Argentine outlaws and fighters, is simply viewing one facet of the tough workingman, an aspect that to the lower class can easily be real but to others may be pure fantasy. In so proceeding, Godoy takes a further step in the direction of poetic Neo-Realism instead of the more limited view of squalor and despair on a single plane. The majority of the novel does portray poverty, fear, and oppression but is mitigated by the more optimistic, open-ended world of Golondrino's intellectual and mythical discoveries.

La cifra solitaria is undoubtedly Godoy's most readable novel in the sense that plot is singular and uniform, characters are fewer and better developed, and Godoy's philosophy of man is more clearly explained than in his other novels. The vocabulary is more universal Spanish and lends itself to easier comprehension and even possibly translation, a feat no one has yet undertaken. Despite these characteristics, this novel alone does not suffice to convey the entire world picture of Angurrientism as a literary style and way of life.

III   *Short Stories*

From 1945 to 1959 Godoy's only published work is a series of short stories. For a study of his literary trajectory the short stories may be taken as representative of this fourteen-year span. There is not, however, any ideological or thematic unity to the six stories. Hence, each will be considered separately. Only two, "El gato de la maestranza" and "L'Herminia se ha vengao," can appropriately be considered as representing the Angurrientist movement, and even the latter is taken verbatim from the author's first novel. The others portray broader segments of humanity. Very likely Godoy realized the possible closed door ahead of any literature promulgating just one social class and made appropriate changes in his literary creation.

"L'Herminia se ha vengao" ("Herminia's Revenge"), also known in other publications as "La venganza de Herminia" ("Herminia's Vengeance") and "Se ahogaron todos los piojos" ("All the Lice Drowned"), relates a brief but pathetically tragic incident in the life of poor Celso and his specter of a wife, Herminia. The skinny wife, who has not tasted meat for weeks, recovers a dead chicken from a filthy drainage ditch, while delousing her hair. Borrowing some added ingredients from neighbors, she prepares a feast for herself and husband. Unable to control her cravings, like any good *angurriento,* she succumbs despite the foul odor, and gorges herself. Later, suffering the painful effects of rotten meat, she drowns in the same ditch that produced the chicken. Godoy ends the story in his typical bizarre, grotesque manner; the unfeeling Celso finds his dead wife and tersely comments: "She got her revenge; all the lice drowned" (87). Once again the author has emphasized improper values and lack of human sentiment. While the story tends to elicit a comic effect, it nevertheless underscores the tragedy of hunger, poverty, and scant regard for human life.

"El gato de la maestranza" ("Cat in the Roundhouse") similarly follows the vein of tragic violence, almost to the same extent as the Spaniard Camilo José Cela's *Tremendista* prose. Workers in the train yards are greeted each day by a friendly black cat which soon becomes a mascot, having a shared meaning to all the laborers. After a short fight with a larger cat, the mascot takes refuge in one of the warm engines. After an extensive search the narrator finds the animal, takes it home, and shares with it his scanty subsistence. Once the cat is nursed back to health, instead of returning it to the train yard, the narrator casually informs us of his new pistol and laconically states, "Bah, I killed the cat" (35). The senseless killing points up man's irrational nature in exterminating that which has most meaning to him. The narrator is not pleased by his action, but the absurdity of life weighed sufficiently heavy on him that it caused the inane death.

Of a more positive nature is "El profesor y unos pelusas" ("The Professor and the Young Rowdies"), forcefully depicting the fleeting joy of Antón, whose students of thirty years fete him for his inspirational life as a teacher. Leaving the bar after all others have departed, he is accosted by a small band of young thieves who knock him down and steal his glasses, money, and identification. Alone on the bridge, Antón rapidly loses faith in youth, contemplating that these may have someday been his students. After returning to their tavern lair, the young robbers are talked and forced into returning all when it is discovered that the victim was a professor. "Teachers make less than I do and I'm blind and lame" (68) observes the organizer of the gang. The stolen articles are returned with an extra bill or two, and the professor gets up from the bridge and goes his way. One cannot help feel the overromanticization of the event and the glorification of the teaching profession. Yet once again Godoy has found a saving grace in the young rowdies, an expression of his "Chilean essence"—respect for education and its mentors. Whether the situation is credible is unimportant; there is honor among thieves, especially when they are poor Chileans dealing with an educator.

A totally different situation is viewed in "Un inspector de sanidad" ("A Public Health Inspector"). The inspector, Andrés, is called to administer medicine to a high government official who has fallen gravely ill and is swollen like a bloated cow. Andrés gives him a shot in his paunch, whereupon the official rouses from his stupor, looks around, and asks, "What, what's, what's happening?" (106). Despite the grieving relatives, the inspector bursts into laughter, unable to contain himself in the realization that the high government official knew nothing when he was considered "a monument of democracy." An hour later the sick man died knowing nothing more or less than he had known all his innocent life. This short story received an excited reception in Chile, for critics and students alike interpreted it as a meaningful artistic criticism of inept government. In its negative evaluation of officialdom it had and still has popular appeal to those of a working class who see no use for ignorant government control. Its merits as a work of art will be reviewed in future chapters.

Certainly Godoy's most polished and perfect short story is "El ramal o el canario bombero" ("The Whip, or The Spouting Canary"). Little known outside of Chile, the story could easily stand alongside the best of Uruguay's Horacio Quiroga as one of the strongest emotional stories of Latin America. An overly sensitive boy, in love with the mountains and nature, has partially tamed a wild canary (somewhat analogous to himself) that spouts water through its beak like a firehose. The child's sensitive spirit is revealed in his frequent illnesses and in the resultant pampering by the maid who overprotects and spoils him. Recently recovered from a mysterious disease, the child attends the birthday party of a rich neighbor, with his canary as his constant and closest friend. The bird is so popular with the wealthy children, who are only acquainted with artificial toys, that the boy narrator is left out of the circle of play. At the party's conclusion he is required to leave his pet for the amusement of the wealthy and unfeeling. After hours of nightmares and anguish, the youth returns to find that his canary has been caged, tormented, and "broken" in his absence. Convinced of the cruelty and complicity of the whole surrounding system, he returns home, angrily hurls the muted bird at his father's feet, and flees to the mountains, alone. An older brother eventually finds him the next day and forces his return home. On the way the child thinks of his father's whip and the inevitable beating he will receive for staying out all night. Gritting his teeth to fortify his valor, he enters the house and sees the whip ready for use. His father demands that he approach, and then the boy records: "He gently held my head. He took me into his heart . . . and chastised my face with the whip of his own tears" (129).

The unexpected ending, so warm and human, is a surprise to the reader as well as to the boy and is illustrative of Godoy's affection for children in his literature. The child, through love and understanding, meshes with the adult world, different from his canary who only received torment from his rich captors.

The familial love and comprehension, so changed from previous Angurrientist literature, draw the reader to the story, creating the sensation of having witnessed a completely universal experience and not simply a rural Chilean happening.

Godoy's final short story, "Sombras" ("Shadows"), published in 1966, is a succinct piece of memorialist literature. While the style is most obviously that of Godoy, the story lacks the emotional involvement of the reader in the material. The death of the author's wife in 1963 left him totally alone, and he often pondered over his own life and whether he had been kind and just to his spouse.[3] In an attempt to eulogize her patience and understanding, Juan wrote "Sombras," discovering that her shadow still remained with him. The main narrative action centers around a neighborhood fire and the love and assistance rendered by this patient woman. To interpret the story in any other fashion than biographical would be unjust to the avowed design of the author.

IV   Sangre de murciélago

The structure of *Sangre de murciélago* (*Bat's Blood*) is strikingly analogous to *Angurrientos*, with its numerous spatial and temporal shifts, its procession of nondeveloped characters, its unity of chapter rather than the whole novel. It is definitely the most autobiographical and takes place within a joint alcoholic-mental treatment institution and its environs. Two principal male characters, Pedro Ordóñez (as sculptor) and the narrator, tie the scattered philosophy and action together; their friendship is the only unifying thread of plot. Each has a lover, Cona for Ordóñez, and Sheva for the narrator. While these lovers are vitally important for the two alcoholics, they are not novelistically significant and could be any women. There are, as well, fifteen or more minor figures, mostly men, confined to the asylum. None is indispensable as an individual; yet all are necessary to the desired atmosphere of the novel. The main figure among these minor characters is Ordóñez' brother-in-law, called "Sangre de murciélago" due to an attempted cure for alcoholism wherein he drank the blood of a bat. The narration of his temporary cure and restoration of youth forms one of the main intercalated stories in the work.

Sangre de murciélago is a novel of dialogue; the heterogeneous characters discourse in milk bars, in the dining rooms of the institution, and even in the bedrooms of numerous female antagonists. The theme is always the same—their own sad condition and their shared outlook on life. Even sex is frequently devitalized in favor of philosophical exposition and essayistic analysis. The action fluctuates between the institution and weekends off in the city. The novel need not be read as a continuous story but must be examined and analyzed for its style and ideas, separately explained and developed. The lack of action and the proliferation of rambling dialogue accurately re-create the asylum where alcoholics and mentally retarded are mixed. The ruined, scandalous past and the useless present lives of the two central figures unite, correspond, until finally both are released from the temporary sanctuary. Both return to their faithful wives, but both keep visiting their more sensual mistresses. In a chance meeting they again begin drinking until Ordóñez is fully saturated. In his drunken state he charges headlong into a moving train. The narrator finds his wife, and together they casually search for the remains of her husband. Although Ordóñez is unquestionably dead, Godoy does not confine him to the earth but rather finds that his brains have ascended upward, into the heavens, giving him a tinge of immortality.

Evident from the earliest part of the novel is the futility of life—no one is fully satisfied or able to carry on satisfactory relationships. Despite some temporary cures, the reader is sure that all the inmates will return to drink or insanity, as indeed both the narrator and Ordóñez do. Hence, one of the major themes growing implicitly from the novel and openly debated by its characters is the problem of existential futility and the inability to effect real progress. Nevertheless, Godoy's men still continue the struggle, still make choices, and still hope in the unattainable future. Despite a tragic end, life is to be lived fully, indulging in wine, sex, and anything else that lends itself to consumption. It is this philosophical concept which links the novel to Godoy's Angurrientist concepts. The characters are most definitely not low-class *rotos*; yet they demonstrate the same inability to plan judiciously, to recognize personal limitations, and to cope with basic problems of life. By creating the world and philosophy of the *roto* among a higher intellectual and social body, Godoy gives broader meaning and application to his ideas and more common ground for his readers. *Angurrien-*

tos and *La cifra solitaria* quite obviously will not be read widely by the social class with which they deal. *Sangre de murciélago*, however, exposes problems and conflicts in harmony with its expected audience.

Sangre de murciélago is Godoy's most complicated novel from the standpoint of structure, style, language, and content. These complications will be examined in future chapters.

V El impedido

During 1967 and 1968 Godoy worked on an elusive manuscript (he left or lost it in several bars and taxis, but it was always thoughtfully returned). The typescript was completed in 1968, and Godoy sought a publisher for *El impedido* (*The Invalid*). Financial help was proffered by friends in the municipality of San Miguel, and when the work appeared, it surprised many who had previously considered his writing completed. The style is unmistakably Godoy's, with poetic flair, intercalation of popular song and verse, and emphasis on a marked prose rhythm. Yet the novel is not disjointed nor divided as in previous works. A single incident unites the entire work—an industrious, thoughtful worker has been injured in an accident and realizes that he will be crippled for an extensive period and sexually impotent. With much solemnity and sincerity he provides a male replacement to satisfy his excitable wife. Natural jealousies, however, finally win out as he sees and hears her involvement with the friend. The triangle, however unlikely, is shattered when the wife's attentions turn from the temporary lover and center on her magnanimous husband. At this juncture he quite unexpectedly regains his masculine health, and order is fully restored to the household. The *nouvelle* is a perfect gem of human concern and understanding. Gone is the pessimistic, somber attitude so prevalent in *Angurrientos*. There is little philosophical or moral preachment, no overglorification of the *roto*, nor any attempt to portray the sufferings of a whole social class. More than in any other novel Godoy has created his own novelistic world rather than attempting a faithful but poetic reproduction of the squalor of the real world. The author has here evolved into a master prose writer, producing an artistic piece with solely artistic purpose, displaying the deepest of human sentiments— love and jealousy.

Godoy's prose production is neither even nor unified. Long lapses of time have passed between one novel and another. He has experimented with many new forms, rarely content to follow any given author or pattern. Some of his prose is of the finest quality in Chile and Latin America; some is highly inferior. The first two novels exhibit a thematic unity—the impoverished but noble life of the *roto*. Around 1950 Godoy expanded his themes to include all social classes, as evidenced by his more recent works. This shift has not enhanced his reputation within Chile, but his more current works are much more accessible to a foreign reading public. The constant throughout his entire production is his stylistic technique of imbuing prose with a myriad of devices which elicit responses in the reader similar to those produced by poetry. So that the reader can more fully comprehend the beauty as well as the meaning of Godoy's prose, these stylistic elements will be carefully described, interpreted, and evaluated in the following chapter, to provide some concrete reasons for calling Godoy a *poetic* Neo-Realist.

CHAPTER 3

Prose Style and Narrative Technique

O NE of the foremost objectives of Juan Godoy was to promote a rich lyric style in prose; he conceives a literature raised from a limited to a universal plane to describe the anguished world of all men. The term "prose style" includes imagery, metaphoric expression, prose rhythm, and other verbal features which assist in determining the poetic qualities of prose. While these elements of style are based on words, words cannot be divorced from meaning: "It is the nature of words to mean. To consider words only as sounds, like drum taps, or to consider written letters as patterned objects, as in alphabet soup, is the same as to consider a Stradivarius as material for kindling."[1] With this concept as a guideline, analysis of style will include not only the accumulation and order of words but their meaning, purpose, evocation, and symbolism as well. The broader aspects of style, which become part of an author's narrative technique, will also be studied and analyzed: point of view, characterization, novelistic structure, narrative rhythm, plot, treatment of time, and space, and so on.

If one passes over these vital aspects of Godoy's prose, he misses the attempt and fulfillment by the author to create lyric expression of a subject heretofore viewed only as gross and lowly. He will tend to view Godoy's work as style for style's sake alone rather than as the creation of the latent poetic nature the writer finds in the *roto*. Hence, before a study of man and his anxieties as expressed in Godoy, one must first comprehend his literary techniques.

I *Imagery—Sensory Impressions*

One of the most distinctive elements of an author's style is his imagery. Images paint the world in which his characters perform and may even shape the lives of those characters. Any expression evoking sensuous appeal may justly be classified as

61

an image. An image in literature will not be seen or heard, as will an image in real life or in painting or music. Words describe an object, a sound, a smell, which must be made sufficiently vivid by the writer to be "imaginable," real, and perceivable by the reader. Based on words, an image as used here is merely the representation through language of sense experience. The writer seeks to express sense experience through language. But he cannot give the reader words alone; he has to evoke conceivable images. This he accomplishes through a sensuous language which rises above everyday speech and description, painting rich images.

Before examining Godoy's imagery, however, a distinction must be made between image and metaphor as studied in this chapter. An image paints a word picture of the concrete, real world of the novel. It is based on perception by the five "standard" senses and on internal sensations such as hunger, thirst, nausea, and the like. It does not allude to anything beyond the description contained in itself. When a writer states, "John is a good-looking, foul-talking, sweet-smelling sailor," he has presented a series of images based on sight (he's handsome), sound (he swears), and smell (he uses cologne). He has described John through a series of images as John is perceived in the concrete world. On the other hand, he may say, "With the face of Adonis, and emitting a fragrance of jasmine, John blasphemed in angry sailor language." In this example he has employed metaphors to enrich his world. Perception is not based solely on sense experience but also upon an understanding of the world alluded to. The metaphor may allude to a historical, literary, philosophical, or psychological world, extending beyond the concrete world of the novel to include broader artistic horizons. John is still handsome, sweet-smelling, and vulgar; but these qualities are perceived through a series of comparisons. The reader knows John is good-looking because he knows of Adonis; he knows John smells pleasant because jasmine is extremely sweet; he knows John swears excessively because he has heard or believes that sailors do. Image and metaphor may mix in a single description: "Although John is handsome and smells like a rose, he swears too freely." For the purposes of this work, image and metaphor will be discussed separately.

The section on metaphor examines the abstract world of allusion and comparison. The study of imagery deals only with the concrete world pictured in the novel itself. Sense impressions —visual, tactile, auditory, gustative, and olfactory—are the basis for imagery, and will be the first concern. Internal sensations, conceptual and synesthetic images will complete the examination. VISUAL IMAGES. Most common among Godoy's images are visual perceptions of the world. In visual images, color very often becomes a significant part of the object described. Schälchly has effected a page-by-page count of *Angurrientos* and has discovered more than 350 references to colors: 67 reds, 54 yellows, 48 blacks, and so on.[2] But when the entire novelistic production is considered (Schälchly wrote before *Sangre de murciélago* and *El impedido* were published), black is the most predominant color in Godoy's imagery. Yellow and red follow closely, however, showing that the world of his novels is richly varied— bright and lively as well as dark and morose. Color is used for esthetic purposes, serving to vivify the created world and to imbue it with precision: "The clear *azure* landscape of the early morning stretched forth her soft dream, her rippled, winged *blue* lake. Pale *bluish* air, savory with the scent of morning stars. The skylights drank the *cerulean* clearness of dawn, lividly *bluing* the room and the things in the room and the sleeping faces"—my italics. *Angurrientos* (111). Five times the pale blue of early morning sky is seen, engulfing a sleeping room. The whole image is one of a still-life painting illuminated with sensuous blue light. A link with the misty blue of *modernista* poetry is evident in this and many other images (*Angurrientos*, 17, 83; *La cifra solitaria*, 13).

Colors in Godoy's created world function to enhance imagery; they bring precision and often symbolic meaning to an image. According to Schälchly, black, red, and yellow account for approximately 55 percent of color images; blues, greens, whites, grays, and the like, complete the world, adding a touch of realism and keeping it from becoming a monotonous cosmos. With such vivid imagery, the novelistic world is as varied as man's everyday experience. Besides standard colors, shadings and blendings vary the images. *Aceitunado, cárdeno, ceroso, cerúleo, cetrino, lívido, oliváceo* are only a few of these often-used "colorful" adjectives.

Visual imagery in Godoy is most frequently a description of nature and landscape. Characters and manufactured goods may be viewed visually, but are more likely to be identified through smell, touch or sound. Man may be dirty and smelly, but the images referring to nature are always of great beauty. Nature is not hostile; it is elegant and inviting, setting a pattern for man to follow. The sky, sun, and mountains are the three objects of nature most frequently wrought into images. Houses and other less noble dwellings are seen through images, containing the preferred adjectives—mossy, filthy, withered, moldy. To these must be added a visual image that appears four times in *Angurrientos*, three in *La cifra solitaria*, twice in the short stories, and twice in the last two novels. *Vigas hollinadas*, sooty beams, appears with such consistency as to be a trademark of Godoy's prose.

Mariano Latorre felt that Godoy's chief contribution to Chilean prose was his original, vivid images.[3] Godoy's visual images are often fresh, unknown in literary antecedents. These he extracted from his own acute observation and poetic sensitivity. One example, of an abandoned locomotive slowly sinking into its self-dug grave, must suffice: "in the empty stomach of a cemetery of unusable locomotives that slowly go down, burying themselves in the earth by their own weight, suffering with rust or turning green with moss and lichen" (*El gato de la maestranza*, 29).

OLFACTORY IMAGES. Visual images set the limits of the created world; smells intensify it. Images relying on the olfactory senses are almost exclusively reserved for people and interiors of edifices in Godoy; nature and the outdoors are seen in different types of images. In other words, the over-all picture is already sketched in visual images; smell, along with taste, touch, and sound, serve to complete the details of the initial sketch.

In descriptions of interiors, smells are usually disagreeable. Manure is the most common of all olfactory sensations in Godoy. Its stench clings to walls, floors, and shoes, as well as to people:

Fouling the air with a yellow stench of manure, a vinegary smell of rotten vegetables, drifting over the nearby stable. (*Angurrientos*, 35)

A smell of chicken excrement, of humidity, of human intimacy, of musty books, and even tobacco, made the atmosphere of the room thicker, oppressive, and indefinite. (*Angurrientos*, 236)

His bare feet fell against the wooden floor and a moldy smell of manure filled the house. (*Angurrientos*, 241)

It [a garbage dump] smelled like moldy old books, like forsaken land, dark, hidden. In my happenings I fell into the trash pile. (*Sangre de murciélago*, 126)

This type of negative olfactory image is common throughout Godoy's prose. Strong stenches overcome any pleasant fragrance that may exist. In sharp contrast to these foul-smelling interiors is the pleasant aroma of the outdoors. "The earth exuded an austere smell, inciting a harmony of herbs and resins" (*La cifra solitaria*, 39). In *La cifra solitaria*, where the blind protagonist is led by a wise dog, smells replace visual images. Golondrino himself is frequently described in terms of his odor rather than of his appearance. Visual images are occasionally used in the novel but to a lesser degree than in others.

Men are always described with negative odors: "His sweaty face stunk of the acid stench of perspiration" (*Angurrientos*, 187, 188). Even the olfactory images referring to women are frequently negative: "In her wake there remained a furrow of appetites and a smell of cheap cream and cologne" (*El gato de la maestranza*, 64). Occasionally more positive olfactory images are employed to describe meals. Food is the sweet-smelling, desirable object of man's existence. The burned milk and sugar image is often repeated in Godoy's initial novel, a delicacy to the hungry poor.

Godoy's olfactory images are not as new or distinct as many of his visual sensations. However, his concern with depicting smells is indicative of a poet's sensitivity to detail. Smells are part of man's real world, and as such must be carried to the created realm of the novel. Although most often negative, they nevertheless enrich and intensify the narration. Godoy does not describe wispy, light, pleasant smells, but heavy, foul smells, unchanging in the passing of time. Imagery shows that the life of the commoner is inextricably linked to stench and filth. Only by approximation to nature can he rise above his condition.

AUDITORY IMAGES. Like olfactory images, Godoy uses sounds to complete the roughly sketched, outline world of visual imagery. Sounds deal with the smaller entities of this world; the larger objects have already been established with visual images. In *Angurrientos* two types of images prevail. First are the images referent to food and its preparation. Instead of seeing or smelling food, an image of the sound it makes while cooking is most common, creating the sensation of closeness and intensity. The narrator is not viewing the world from a distance; he is directly involved in it. He is so close to his world that he hears even the minutest sounds, "a deaf echo," "a strange silence." The sound of food cooking emphasizes the desire for physical satisfaction in the life of the commoner: "And the near-empty frying pans began to hum their pathetic unchangeable tune of poverty" (*Angurrientos*, 9). The most illustrative auditory image occurs when several poor workers arrive home and discover a prepared goose. No visual or olfactory image is provided, only the sound: "Immediately it began to *sizzle* over the ashes" (176).

The second class of auditory imagery in the first novel is the sound of animals and the smaller creatures of nature. Cows bellow, dogs bark, frogs croak, birds sing, chickens cackle, stream-, lets trickle in one paragraph: "Frogs croaked in Salto Lagoon. Overripe fruit, loosed from the branches, burst on the ground with a spongy splat. The trill of water in ditches. From a tall, sleepy cottonwood the laugh of a sparrow hawk fell to the ground ..." (127). The entire scene is depicted through a series of beautiful auditory images. Nature relates freely with man and is as significant a part of the world as are people. Through imagery, Godoy mixes nature and man; they share a common existence. Naturally there is much sound imagery which does not fit into the two categories already mentioned. Man makes sounds—footsteps, snoring, singing, for example—but this type is much less frequent than auditory images of food and the smaller entities in nature.

La cifra solitaria, however, does not fit into the pattern, and must be considered separately. Sound imagery plays a role equal to that of smell in the novel. The keenly developed auditory sense of Golondrino, the blind soothsayer, is reflected throughout the narration in an abundance of sound imagery unknown in Godoy's other novels. Sound imagery compensates for lack of vision. Golondrino himself is first introduced by sounds: "The *silence* mortified with its tense arc of anguish.... Beyond the house, measured *beats*, isochronously spaced, *echoed* in the walls and doors, drawing nearer: toc...toc...toc... toc.... The cane taps passed through the wall, through the door, through us.... The tapping faded, finally, in the distance" my italics. (*La cifra solitaria*, 25, 27). Throughout the remainder of the narration, Golondrino's appearances are always preceded by his characteristic "toc... toc... toc." He is a character who sees, and is seen, through sounds.

During the dramatic wake held for Serafín, visual images disappear, and such unnerving sounds of sobbings and throat-clearings are granted prime importance in the narration. This technique convincingly reproduces a death wake, where vision is often blurred, and all senses except sound are dulled or absent. Godoy's auditory images in this section are the most lucid and easily perceived of his entire creation: "A short *silence* followed in whose depths the *deaf murmur* of the rain united. Women's *sobs* interspersed by men *clearing their throats* as they contemplated their cosmic grief. Composed of remote solicitudes, the piercing *voice* of Golondrino: 'Hail Mary, Full of Grace...'" my italics. (72). After Golondrino's entreating prayer, all remain silent. But suddenly a new auditory image interrupts the momentary hush: "In the patio, Tocante hammered the coffin.... His hammer blows resounded like heartbeats of death" (72). Throughout the remainder of the wake the regular, upsetting, hypnotic hammer blows pound like the beat of a heart. They function as a metronome background for the pseudoreligious ceremony that follows. The lights are even turned out, so that only sounds prevail. Golondrino chants; the ministering body barks back his magic words; sobs break the occasional silence; the widow frantically taps the floor; a distant locomotive hisses its serpentlike interruption; a clap of thunder terrorizes the frightened congregation; and the incessant hammer blows continue, as Golondrino's hypnotic voice drones on. As the dramatic chant concludes and the devil is defeated, silence settles for a brief moment, only to be broken by the image-filled finale: "The lower jaw of the dead man flapped open with an amphibious *clatter*. 'God has saved him,' cried Chopi, *sobbing*. 'God has saved him,' *responded* the chorus like a *deaf silence*, getting up, sighing deep relief. A *murmur* of dresses, a *stamping* of stiff bones..." my italics. (83). During the entire scene only one visual image is recorded—a black widow spider that descends from the ceiling to the dead man's forehead. All the rest are vivid auditory impressions.

A similar scene occurs in the final section of *Angurrientos*. Eulogio, the young child in bed, had previously been aware of visual images only. He blew out his candle and suddenly experienced new sensations. First internal feelings, so vital in Godoy, appear—feelings of smoothness and restfulness. Then, in the heavy darkness, auditory images invade his senses: dogs barking, the distant sea, a neighbor's door shutting (240, 241). The boy's fear magnifies the night sounds until no other sensations are experienced. Only the appearance of a friendly man alleviates the anguish.

In this example and the scene from *La cifra solitaria,* Godoy heightens dramatic suspense by eliminating all but one sensory impression. In this way a deeper, more intensive penetration into the sense images is achieved, bringing the reader into intimate contact with the created world.

TACTILE IMAGERY. Godoy's narrators are close to, and present in, the world they describe. Rather than describe through visual images observed from a distance, they enjoy an intimacy with their character, depicting sounds, smells, and tactile sensations. The predominant tactile image is coldness. Trees, birds, people, the sky, clouds, houses, and countless other objects are characterized by cold. Nothing escapes the chill; nature as well as people share its misery. Its overfrequent use is suggestive of the miserable, deficient life of the poor. The images dealing with cold are hard, concrete images of an unchangeable, incomprehensible world. Frequently the images become metaphoric and will be discussed as such in the appropriate section of this chapter. Women are the exception; in images they are warm and soft and provide refuge from the hard world of cold objects.

Related to cold is the imagery surrounding rain. Rain frequently causes or intensifies the cold. In all of Godoy's novels and in three short stories, rain is dominant. Rain imagery is occasionally auditory but is usually tactile. An auditory image indicates that the listener is comfortably inside a dwelling; the *roto* more frequently feels the rain, without protection. In contrast to the harsh sensations of cold and rain imagery are the images evoking softness and smoothness: "A soft, silky shadow, at angles with the clouds..." (*Angurrientos,* 96).

CONCLUSION. Godoy's prose, replete with sensory impressions, is richer by far than the Criollist literature of the previous generation. It abounds with greater imagery than even his contemporaries, not only in quantity, but in quality. Quality, in the case of an image, is measured by its vividness, by its ability to be mentally reproduced by the reader. As is evident from the above examples, Godoy's near faultless handling of the language does create striking, conceivable images for the reader. Narrative technique and plot organization are seldom as closely worked as are poetic images. By basing his writing so heavily on imagistic language, Godoy brings a strong poetic tone to his prose.

Godoy has often been compared with Spain's Gabriel Miró for his exquisite sensitivity and his detailed description of intricate, intimate objects. The similarity is correct, but no direct influence exists, as discussed in the first chapter. While Godoy does sketch and outline his world with visual imagery, he relies heavily on tactile, olfactory, and auditory images for the polished details of the picture. In this way the reader is brought into intimate, personal contact with the created world, since he must be present to touch, smell, and hear. The minute details depicted by these three senses create precise poetic images.

Images in Godoy generally refer to the concrete, objective world. Though usually handled with poetic subjectivity, they nevertheless evoke an identifiable object. The objects and sounds of nature are the first and most commonly imagized.

Second in frequency are images referring to sex, especially female sex organs. Some critics would even place sex imagery ahead of nature.[4] Sex imagery is not vulgar but is often ennobling and beautiful: "Her sex a fire like a jeweled member, of silken semidarkness, of gold, fleshy..." (*Sangre de murciélago*, 167).

As in drama, where the monologue is replete with poetic imagery, so in Godoy the narrator's descriptions abound in sensuous language. The paucity of images in dialogue contrasts with their abundance when the narrator alone has the stage. It is he who creates and interprets images for the reader. He painstakingly sets the stage for each scene before moving on with the narration. The narrator's presence in Godoy's works raises prose from commonplace description to elevated, dramatic poetry.

II *Metaphor—Technique and Meaning*

Though precise and beautiful, Godoy's images alone are insufficient to penetrate to the depth of his novelistic world. Sight, smell, and sound do not capture all of man's experience; therefore, Godoy uses metaphor to enrich meaning in his literary universe. Through metaphor he carries the reader from the perceptual world of images to the evocative, unseen sphere of association, comparison, and analogy. Past mixes with present, literature with science, real life with myth, man with nature— all through the use of metaphor.

The simple definition of metaphor as the substitution of one thing for another, or the identification of two things, illustrates the dualistic nature of this figure of speech. Metaphor is a type of comparison or identification between two objects, ideas, people, and so on. The first half of the metaphor is an *image*, conceivable in the mind of the reader. It is the aspect which I. A. Richards has called "vehicle," and it may be a man, a mountain, a mood, or an idea. It provides the basis for the identification. The second part of the metaphor is the *idea* (Richards calls it "tenor") which is associated with the initial image. It enriches the image by adding original, non-"imageable" depth. It joins two objects that the reader would normally not associate. The term "idea" as used for this second part of metaphor may be misleading. It is not necessarily an abstract concept; it may also be a material object which is not usually associated with the first image in reality. When Godoy says, "Nico took up the woman in his husky *arms* of *trees*," my italics, both the image or vehicle (arms) and the idea or tenor (trees) are concrete images. Arms and trees both exist in man's world of experience but are not logically associated with each other. The latter creates the metaphor and evokes the poetic idea; interaction between image and idea provides metaphorical meaning.

Many critics have elaborately classified different types of metaphors,[5] but such an exercise adds nothing to meaning, at least in Godoy. More important, and necessary to the study, is the subject of the metaphor, and the meaning evoked in the *idea*. The *image* refers to the concrete, perceptible world and has already been examined in Godoy's imagery. It is the *idea* and the effect upon the *image* which demands critical analysis. Herein, the emphasis will be on the meaning of metaphor, seen through interaction of *idea* and *image*.

HUMANIZATION. Throughout his entire novelistic production, Godoy breathes human life into all that is not human. Nature, animals, and inanimate objects are endowed with characteristics normally reserved for man. So frequent is this technique that not a single page of Godoy's writings is free of humanization. Several examples will be examined in detail. "On his knees

Matías caressed the blond beauty of the guitar" (*Angurrientos,* 92); "someone stole a laugh from the sleeping harp" (*Angurrientos,* 118). Godoy gives life to musical instruments. The blond guitar is caressed; the harp sleeps, until someone wakes her and elicits laughter from her strings. In the first work, more than any other novel, music is an important part of the narration. The popular songs and dances in the novel are usually accompanied by instrumentation, and these instruments are given the same fullness of life enjoyed by the human participants. In these examples humanization builds until, in a room of dancing, singing, swinging workers, nothing remains inanimate.

Of all nonhuman objects imbued with qualities of man, wine is one of the most frequently metaphorized. It usually laughs, but may dance or play. Never sad, wine always evokes happiness. In *Sangre de murciélago,* humanized wine looms so important as to be one of the principal characters of the story. In a double metaphor the reader experiences "white wine laughing with its golden snails." The snails are the effervescent bubbles that move like sprites through the liquor. The second metaphor enhances the first, creating a visual image of laughing wine.

During daylight hours, Godoy contents himself with describing cities in images. But after dark the city comes to life through metaphor and participates in the joys and crimes of night. In the novel the city is seen as a woman, but not just an ordinary female. Santiago is an "ugly, hostile woman, overpious and mustached" (93). Besides humor, the metaphor has balanced complexity.

Frequently given human characteristics are periods of the day. Morning is a fresh, waking woman, while evening is usually a man: "Squeezed her breasts like bouquets of light the dawn wrapped in mountains" (*Angurrientos,* 61); "the wind snatched the hair from the sun, leaving it bald and pure, looking like a man wrapped up in himself, shaking" (*Angurrientos,* 83). The above examples further illustrate the complex nature of Godoy's metaphors. Through humanization, morning and evening are more than temporal units; they become participants in the novelistic action. Morning is sensual and behaves accordingly. Evening speaks and shares in the lives of the characters.

Similar to periods of the day, seasons of the year are given human qualities. The humanization of seasons provides some of the author's best and most sustained metaphors, all stemming from a single image. Springtime is the most common season so humanized (*Sangre de murciélago,* 30, 49, 218).

Nature, in her myriad forms, is constantly assuming humanity's attributes. Mountains, trees, and water, in that order of frequency, are portrayed with many of man's characteristics. As indicated in a previous section, nature is alive and eternal and is able to participate as a character. She has a direct effect on the lives of those who know and love her: "A giant medlar tree, with broad *feet,* fatherly *arms* and *hair* anointed with oil and burnished by the winds, all jelled with bouquets of gold and sweetness, rocked me in my infancy" . . . my italics. (*La cifra solitaria,* 10). Nature is warm, friendly, and inviting. She always accepts man when he is rejected by the cold human world. Her softness is revealed through the figures of speech with which she is described. One of Godoy's most beautiful metaphors presents a vivid image, blending the natural world with humanity. So successful was it in his first novel, that he altered it slightly and used it again: "The *fire* closed her ashen eyelids" (*Angurrientos,* 141). "The charcoal covered itself with ashes, like forgotten thoughts" (*La cifra solitaria,* 53). In both instances, burning embers are given the spark of life (eyelids, thoughts) and then cover themselves with ashes as they die. The first trope, particularly, produces a beauty rarely achieved in prose.

Godoy's technique of humanization through metaphor brings life and movement to a world that man ordinarily sees as static and inanimate. Man is not the sole actor on a motionless stage but is surrounded by objects that speak, sing, dance, and dream —by objects which are not only acted upon but which themselves act. The joyful life of the entire world creates movement, constant shift, and change of mood in the narration. The ambient is no longer concrete and objective, but is now subjective, due to its human qualities. By humanizing wine, the city, periods of time, nature, and so forth, Godoy changes the reality of these entities. Still possessing their inherent properties, they are blessed with new and deeper characteristics.

Of course, humanization, or personification, is a traditional technique in poetry. As such, its extensive use by Juan Godoy is another of his conscious efforts to break up the patterns of straightforward narration and bring poetry to the fore. All that surrounds man is alive and must be granted equal expression and development.

AMPLIFICATION OF MAN. Just as Godoy may imbue nature and natural objects with human characteristics, so may his created characters share in the natural world. In Godoy, man possesses traits normally reserved for plants and animals. Some would immediately call this technique dehumanization or animalization. But a careful examination discloses a man who is no less human because he has animallike characteristics; rather, his reality is ampified to include all his surroundings. Man not only wanders through but becomes a participant in nature.

That Godoy's characters are no less human for their comparison to the plant and animal world is easily perceived through the descriptive characterization of Coralia, a dramatic figure of "Un inspector de sanidad." To represent this enchanting figure, the narrator finds mere imagery insufficient; hence, he employs various metaphoric comparisons: "Coralia, gracious and delicate like a *pistil*" (91). "Her loose hair, of golden *iridescence,* like a *broken wave…*" my italics. (91). "The reflections gave to the face of my lover a translucent quality, a *porcelain* effect" my italics. (91). "Her eyelids slept like the flower of thought" (92). "My lover laughed and her smile opened like a great delicate flower" (96). "She wiggled the tip of her nose, like the abdomen of a bee sucking honey from a flower" (96). Coralia is the image, the basis for the metaphor. Around her the narrator weaves ideas that enhance her beauty and draw her closer to nature. Three times she is equated with a graceful flower, in traditional metaphors that show a conformity to classical poetic norms. Her rainbow-hued hair is of gold, signifying value as well as beauty. Her loose hair is a wave, flooding her neck and breaking over her shoulders. A white, halolike forehead is equated with pure snow, and her unblemished face with fine porcelain. The only disconcerting characteristic is the nervous wiggle of her nose, but even this is rhythmic and sensual like the pulsations of a bee seeking nectar.[6] In her collation with nature, Coralia is ennobled rather than dehumanized. Her beauty is the beauty of nature, never artificial. Godoy amplifies the spheres of reality and endows his character with all the positive qualities of her natural surroundings.

Even when characters assume more negative properties from their environs, they are not dehumanized. In the same short story, two men, the Inspector and the "Important Dignitary," repeatedly appear in metaphor, always negatively (94-106).

However, apelike, bestial, or devilish man may appear at a given moment, Godoy takes care to keep him from remaining so. Included in man's nature are all characteristics of lower life, but even in the most negative examples Godoy manipulates metaphor to amplify human reality rather than destroy or debase it.

The most frequently misinterpreted character from Godoy's prose is blind Golondrino. The appellation itself, a swallow, is presumed by many to denote dehumanization and beastlike qualities. Further, Golondrino himself states: "Ah, my lord, man is an ox.... I am an ox. Since I've forgotten my name and am now an ox, I am now simply Golondrino" (*La cifra solitaria*, 29). But Golondrino is never depicted as a beast in the novel's metaphors; he is likened to positive, religious concepts. He enjoys the elevated position of prophet among the men with whom he walks. His "man is an ox" assertion, true synecdoche, is immediately clarified by a poetic insertion, symbolically eulogizing the ox tongue: "Oh, what pain leads the ox to his destiny!" (31). Man and ox are similar only in that they share in anxiety over an unknown destiny. Rather than being a degrading quality, the similarlity is merely an expression of anguish, of a desire to transcend terrestrial limitations. Throughout the novel Golondrino is metaphorically aggrandized and dignified until he is finally allowed to leave earth without tasting of death; he is not an ox, a beast of burden; he is a demigod.

As Godoy amplifies man's reality, the sea is the most common tenor. Since the theme of his works has really nothing to do with the sea, such references may appear to be a stylistic anomaly, until one carefully observes that such terms are usually parts of a metaphor. Man is part of, or like, the sea in myriad ways. This metaphoric use of the sea occurs in all Godoy's prose: "My cousin Alberto enjoyed [sexually] a thick, *stormy sea* with Chabela. The *boat* which the *waves* brought in is still in the *cove*," my italics, meaning that he is still visiting the young lady (*Angurrientos*, 23). "Eulogio, stern as the sea..." (*Angurrientos*, 28). "His beard *breaking* like a hoary *wave* upon his chest" my italics (*Angurrientos*, 213). "Her loose hair... like a broken *wave*" my italics (*El gato de la maestranza*, 91). As a comparative idea, the sea has been a poetic image for centuries. Poets have considered it as the source of life, as well as the final resting place into which man's river must flow.

Although in recent years the sea has become a symbol of anguish and alienation,[7] in Godoy the sea generally represents constancy, rest from earthly care, peace. Equation with the sea exalts man from being a lowly earth creature to being a noble partaker of the eternities. It amplifies man to the infinite. Like the sea, Godoy's men are always changing in outward appearance; yet they are always the same in their basic character. Man is eternalized by use of this traditional poetic symbol. Specifically, it is most often the female who is represented by the sea. She is man's haven and rest. Her anatomy inspires repeated, often crude, metaphor. "A whole *eddy* of *algae* opened ... perhaps Wanda would loose her restless youth in the *crashing waves*. And in reality, her breasts *flowed* smoothly when she walked" my italics (*Angurrientos,* 23).

Man's collation with the animal or natural world is usually positive. He has arms like tree branches because trees are strong and durable. He may possess qualities of a cow or horse because these animals exemplify resistance to suffering, a strength which man must likewise acquire. When man assumes characteristics of iron or wood, it is not to extinguish his humanity. Rather, his reality is amplified to include the affirmative aspects of wood or iron. Man may occasionally bellow, for a strong, commanding voice is a positive trait.

At the opposite end of the spectrum are certain negative qualities which Godoy attributes to man. These are generally couched in humor and must not be taken as serious dehumanization.

In summary, Godoy amplifies human existence to include all parts of the surrounding world. Man is ennobled and not dethroned by sharing with nature. Woman is compared with the sea and is man's eternal haven.

CONCLUSION. Godoy's metaphoric technique abounds with complexities. Occasionally he avails himself of simile and simple metaphor, where there is but one point of resemblance. But compound (various points of similarity) and complex (one identification built upon another) metaphors are more characteristic of his style. A few of his metaphors become so involved as to require research and explanation to decipher them: "The horn rent the drowsiness of the sulking air, tinted by misty sun" (*Angurrientos,* 66). "Lonely beings, casting no shadow, and in whose minds birds of frozen fire harbored" (*Sangre de murciélago*, 16). Fortunately, this type of complexity is minimal.

Juan Godoy is sometimes charged with undue and irresponsible use of metaphor. Chief among critics has been Pedro Selva ("Alone") who describes Godoy's generation as living under the "tyranny of the metaphor."[8] The charge against his use of metaphor is not one of inferior quality; rather, it is of excessive quantity. Too many metaphors, it is argued, weaken the plot and destroy continuity. But the point Pedro Selva has failed to grasp is that Godoy's metaphors are not merely decorative; they are expressive. The function of metaphor in the novelist's work is to bring an inanimate world to full life, to give vitality to all man's surroundings. Man, too, participates in the processes of the natural world. Therefore, if metaphors are excessive, it is because the creator sees an abundant blending and sharing by man and nature. There can be no doubt that Godoy is a great stylist and that the cornerstone of his style is metaphor. While his works abound in metaphor, there is no abuse. Expression preempts decoration.

The world of concrete images is not sufficient to depict Godoy's created universe. No amount of direct description can inform the reader of Golondrino's pain and anguish. Only through metaphoric comparison to the condemned ox are the depths of his soul exposed. Godoy uses metaphor to penetrate the unseen, the indescribable. Only through relating the unseen world of association and allusion with the narrative world of the novel can Godoy achieve the depth he desires.

An examination of the ideological sources of Godoy's metaphors discloses inspiration from the land itself. Only in *Sangre de murciélago* are symbols from previous literature used extensively to form the tenor for the metaphor. But even in this novel nature provides the basis for most comparisons. Man unites with nature, and nature responds with humanlike behavior. As an astute observer of man's environs, Godoy takes images familiar to all, poeticizes them through comparison to nature, and produces an intriguing metaphor. The sea, with all its poetic tradition, is the major source of comparison. Godoy also uses nature to poeticize man; its telluric effect is strengthened in numerous metaphors. Metaphor is not an escape from reality but rather a deeper penetration into it, to the point that nature and man unite.

Godoy's first novel, written at the age of twenty-six, is the richest in metaphors. While there is no paucity in his other novels, *Angurrientos* is the most heavily endowed. At that young age Godoy had already conceived his plan for literary creation and had worked and reworked his initial creation into a mature style.

Metaphor is the basis for poetic prose.[9] Godoy knows its worth in raising the novel from imagistic description of a confined locale, to poetic expression of an entire continent. Metaphor in Godoy brings sensuous experience, even deeper than that of imagery, to prose. Further, it is a means of concentration, a way of saying much in brief compass. Metaphor in Godoy heightens the poetic nature of the prose by involving the reader in imaginative pleasure. The reader himself delights in conceptualizing words into pictures. It is Godoy's mastery of metaphor which exalts his prose and earns it a place among the best of Latin American novels.

III *Symbolism*

While words symbolize objects and ideas and convey meaning, they may also express more subtle, implied meanings. For example, every reader understands the command, "close your eyes"; but when Godoy states that "men die . . . and still they haven't opened their eyes," the reader perceives that in certain contexts *eyes* imply understanding and wisdom. Symbolism may be defined as the representation of a reality on one level of reference by a corresponding reality on another. For example, eyes, an anatomical term, symbolize understanding, a spiritual concept. Without proper definition, confusion could result in distinguishing metaphor and symbol. Metaphor is a type of comparison, composed of idea and image. Meaning arises from the interaction of the two segments. Symbol, conversely, lacks the implied comparison. The two elements of symbol do not interact to create the final idea; meaning springs from implication. When an author regularly employs a word, image, or metaphor throughout an entire novel, or in all his works, it assumes characteristics of a symbol. A metaphor used for the first time is likely to be just a metaphor. But if the same figure of speech is reiterated several times, it usually becomes symbolic.

Symbols in Godoy frequently center around man, his spiritual inabilities, his emotional state, and his anguish. They may also represent the type of world in which he subsists. Although symbolism in Godoy's early works has been capably studied,[10] several additional symbols from later works are here examined.

Through continual reference, eyes express symbolic meaning in Godoy. Mention of eyes is not always symbolic; description of eyes may be a simple image or a complex metaphor. While some references are simple description, the majority are both descriptive and symbolic. Connotative recurrence extends meaning from the descriptive to the symbolic level. Schälchly has counted the number of times references to eyes appear in Godoy; ninety-eight in the first novel, fifty-four in the second, and twenty-one in the short stories of El gato de la maestranza. The same proliferation extends to Sangre de murciélago and El impedido.

In Godoy, eyes connote and symbolize emotional state. Rather than declare that: "John was fiery mad," the narrator merely observes and describes John's expressive, symbolic eyes: "A fiery glow blazed in John's eyes." Thus, the eyes become the means through which the reader is apprised of John's inner being. Revelation of man's interior through outward symbols is another of Godoy's methods of penetrating the human soul. Not only do eyes symbolically reveal emotions, they also bring forth that which is invisible to physical description. "He shook the girl who rolled her alcoholic green eyes" (Angurrientos, 47). "He spit the beam from his eye...and it [the eye] filled with a flock of shadowy twigs" (Angurrientos, 83). "I could say so many things about the white of the eye: it is a cornea effect, a fishbone, the hollowness of snow in the rock of anguish, white slime around dead waters, a mutilated light.... That whiteness of the fallen star, whiteness the color of death" (Sangre de murciélago, 108).

Eyes in Godoy also symbolize a search for spiritual light and truth. Golondrino, from the author's second novel, is physically blind but is the only one in his world who possesses true spiritual existence. Most men close their eyes to spiritual value. Animals possess it. Mortal man does not; his open eyes are symbolic of his blindness. The wise, legendary Golondrino, on the other hand, "leads a double existence. His eyes shut forever, his spirit replaces them and taps along in the immensity of the universe, discovering truth, the irreality of life, and the terrible truth of death."[11] At Golondrino's departure, the child-narrator realizes his own blindness: "We all see with mortal eyes...and we're blind. He, he who was blind, has seen the light, the source of light which we will never see" (*La cifra solitaria*, 106).

Related to eye symbolism is light symbolism. The eye, entrance to the soul, receives and may also give forth light. Through all of Godoy, light assumes connotations of goodness, truth, cleanliness, and innocence. The association of light and truth is biblical symbolism: "I am the light of the world: he that followeth me shall not walk in darkness, but shall have the light of life" (John 8:12). The challenge is for man to cast out inner darkness and give place to pure light: "Wanda was an acrid bud of light in an obscure corner of his heart. And her soul had kissed him with the soft spring of light in the immense soul of the world" (*Angurrientos*, 237). Wanda, like Golondrino, possesses truth and meaning (light) within her own soul. The outer world, in Godoy, is dark and tenebrous; light must originate from within. An effulgent morning brings memory of innocent childhood to Ordóñez. Light penetrates his soul to call forth cleanliness, goodness, and truth, in the only unbeguiled period of his life (*Sangre de murciélago*, 124). Throughout the novel Ordóñez avidly searches for meaning in life. As the narration concludes he realizes that only death can bring lasting truth and, hence, directs himself toward a symbolic light—that of a train. Only in suicide does the sculptor attain light or truth.

Despite eyes like frozen craters, blind Golondrino is able to see light, the symbolic light of spiritual truth. His search is completed. At midnight he sits at the trunk of a mythical fig tree, awaiting the entrance of light. He experiences a new vision of glorious light and then dies. Light is the symbol of truth and goodness. Absence or extinguishment of light symbolizes decease or impending death. Immediately after Augusto's death in *Angurrientos* the only light in the house, a candle, "burns down into an old can" until it finally fades completely. Serafín, from the second novel, is wounded in a dimly lit bar, dies, and is installed in an unilluminated chamber. Smothering of light at death is also characteristic in the short stories (*El gato de la maestranza*, 35; "Sombras," 52).

In contrast to the dark, somber endings where death is present are *Sangre de murciélago* and *La cifra solitaria*. In both instances the central figure is transformed without tasting of death. Ordóñez, drawn by the magnetic headlight of the train, runs toward it, hypnotized. His intelligence ascends upward, toward a brilliant star. The symbolism of light is particularly vivid in the case of Golondrino, who proceeds upward, filled with the eternal light from heaven (106).

A third recurring symbol, seen in many of the illustrations already cited, is the word *root*. Roots symbolize origin, primitive force, and telluric ancestry. Like the two preceding symbols, this one also relates closely to man. The human race is rootless, torn, and severed from telluric values. Man has become an aimless wanderer, attempting to regain his past origins. The search for foundation or source resembles man's quest for light. While the search for light leads man heavenward, roots direct him toward the earth. Through examination of his past and present life and comprehension of his ancestry, man may discern the roots of life. Once discovered, they will grant solidarity and purpose to existence. Man will no longer be tossed to and fro by every wind of doctrine. The "truth" Edmundo seeks is nothing more than identity, an understanding of roots. Golondrino is the only figure who actually discovers and lives according to primal impulses. The two narrators of *Sangre de murciélago* spend the entire novel searching for identity in a disordered world. Tragically it is only in death that Godoy's characters attain understanding of their roots. As Ovalle lies dying, "A raucous subterranean current flowed to his heart, pounding, unmercifully, like sap emerging from deep millennial roots" (222).[12] Ordóñez suffers a similar lot; after a fruitless quest, he finds fulfillment only in death. One of the anguished characters of *Sangre de murciélago* "kneeled down and gently kissed the field, trapping the grass with his ear to listen to the sound of the planet" (29). Earth's roots emit sounds, messages to mankind. Horacio reminds his bar partners of their uprooted nature: "We have no roots, no roots at all.... The Spaniards planted the seeds of culture in ashes of extermination" (*Angurrientos*, 131).

The character who achieves fullest understanding in Godoy's prose is Golondrino. Social, psychological, and political philosophies play no role in his life. He has found his ancestral roots and is guided by telluric powers. Through interiorization and concentration, he reaches inner light and thus discovers himself.

Through understanding of his own roots and perceiving divine light and truth, he attains immortality. Three times mention is made of the "root of life," which complete's man's being. Golondrino lives because he nurtures the mystical union between man, nature, and God.

Ashes symbolize the passing of time. The metaphor of a fire covering itself with ashes has already been illustrated. Ashes signify a lapse of time from the previous narration. Ashes, or ash color, symbolize approaching old age. Augusto's age is indicated by his hair (*Angurrientos*, 18). "There below," states Golondrino, "is a little mountain of ashes, and I am a bright spot, persisting, casting black smoke into the abyss..." (43). Ashes symbolize the finite, the temporal. They revolve around man and appear as an indication of the instability of life.

Contrasting with the ash symbol is that of the *sky*, which signifies eternity, freedom, and vastness. While earth may impose limitations, freedom from time and anguish is obtained in the upward glance. Man is somehow capable of transcending time. While many references to the sky occur in poetic description and are simple images, others are charged with symbolic meaning for the characters of the novel (*Angurrientos*, 82; *La cifra solitaria*, 38, 106).

In addition to its constant metaphoric use, the *sea*, and water in general, assume symbolic meaning in Godoy. Ideas symbolized by water vary according to context; most common are peace, love, anguish, and strength. When there is a woman involved in the immediate passage, references to the sea usually symbolize tranquillity, or at least a rest from the mental torments: "Alejandro swung his heart in rhythm to that salty rump, where her thighs frolicked with a soft sea-like roll" (*Angurrientos*, 16). Besides the concept of woman as peace and haven, the sea is also a symbol of love and eroticism. Woman's anatomy is symbolized with sea terms, as has already been discussed.

The sea also symbolizes anguish and the anxieties of finite existence. Man is limited; he yearns for the timeless expanse of the sea.[13] In other instances, the sea is a symbol of strength and power. Augusto's brow has the strength of a roaring sea. A herd of oxen advance like the incoming tide. Ordóñez' stare has the force of a breaking wave. Golondrino's spiritual capacities are repeatedly equated with the sea. As the sightless philosopher departs from earth, he unites with the strength of the sea and the eternities of the sky.

Man's pain, tragedy, and inability to alter destiny are represented in the symbol of the *ox*. Already cited was Golondrino's self-imposed metaphor in which he compares himself with the ox. The symbol also occurs in the first novel, but is absent from other works: "the tongue of an ox, hanging, lonely.... A whistle directs the ox toward death, a rough snare, a broken will. Oh, how much pain leads the ox to his fate" (*La cifra solitaria*, 31).

After a drinking bout and a fight with his wife, Serafín, the slaughterer, waxes compassionate; he can no longer bear to kill the ox. Serafín is Godoy's most vivid example of pain and unalterable destiny. While he butchers the ox he experiences the suffering of the beast. The two beings blend in an inseparable, symbolic union.

Beginning with *Angurrientos* and increasing in intensity through *El impedido*, wine is a dominant symbol; in fact, it becomes the unifying thread of the narrative. It symbolizes irrationality, emotions dominating reason, and truculence. "Wine is a brutal urgency, an impulse toward incomplete suicide."[14] Religious connotations of wine as a purifier, as the blood of Christ, are infrequent. Godoy turns to Greek and Latin mythology for the symbolic base. Bacchus and Dionysus, with the accompanying symbolism of pleasure, poetic inspiration, mystic rapture, and vitality, are present in the works. But Godoy does more than merely adopt classical symbols; he adds to them. Wine, as shown in the study of metaphor, is frequently humanized and given power. It dominates intellect and testifies to man's irrational nature. By linking classical mythology with his own observations, Godoy creates an original symbol, expressive of his Angurrientist philosophy. If man were rational, he would not drink to excess. But man lacks reason, and so he drinks. Wine is the symbol of this irrationality.

Ovalle's wife refuses to drink, but "a spider glass of wine moved its viscous legs toward the woman" (*Angurrientos*, 88). Her refusal to drink is interpreted as triumph of reason over emotion, killing the deadly spider. Wine is the symbol of Edmundo's injudicious abandonment of "truth"; he falls into drink and utters the incoherencies of the novel's final paragraphs. Serafín is normally a sensitive, sorrowing soul, except when under the spell of wine: alcohol "takes hold, throws him into a vertigo of bloody, deified wine, of violence and poetry, and finally slipping into the terror of primitive slime" (60).

Bat's blood is Godoy's original metaphor to express the irrational effects of wine. The first hundred pages of the novel report the conversation of incurable alcoholics, their eulogies and condemnations of drink. Much of the discussion itself lacks reason and organization. Here, more than in other novels, classical mythology is associated with wine symbolism: "Suddenly, taken by an irresistable sense of good health—in a trance of mythomania—he perforated the air with a chilling screech, and grabbing a dry branch, his thyrsus, let loose the war cry of Bacchus" (49). Following the war cry, the young Véliz explains the classical symbolism of wine. Even though quite accurate, his lengthy discourse convinces the listeners of his insanity; wine has destroyed his reason.

Wine is also a symbol of man's union with telluric powers. As man drinks, he symbolically fuses with the land, becoming part of his native soil. Wine exalts man by extending his life into the history, conflicts, and traditions of his land. This symbolism, even more than the previously discussed irrationality, evokes the cult of Bacchus and Dionysus:

Therefore, wine in skins is the best expression of a culture, and its nature. (*Angurrientos,* 170)

Our Chile speaks of creative wines and *chichas,* wines that make humanity. The birth of Dionysus, the god of wine in Greece, is linked to the identification of nectar and semen. His orgies are erotic. (*Sangre de murciélago,* 48)

fields bursting with fruit trees and vineyards, their heads bowed by the weight of the great ripe boughs, dripping like the breasts of the earth. (*Sangre de murciélago,* 84)

Wine is not evil. In excess it subverts reason; in moderation it is holy and ennobling. Problems stem from the appetite of the *angurriento* who does everything in excess. "*Vinus opus Dei, ebrietas opus daemonis*" (*Angurrientos,* 51).

The *mirror* symbolizes man's subconscious mind and incomprehension of self. A mirror returns a true image of physical mien, but this is not sufficient for Godoy. Physical reality is partial and deluding. Hence, man must look beyond the mirror, or into several mirrors, to find himself. Edmundo's "great expres-

sion," his summary of life, is that man does not behold himself
in his totality. He only comprehends a minute part of his being.
Yet life is not complete unless the whole is understood. To
resolve this problem, man must go beyond the mirror. Nacha,
from *La cifra solitaria*, beholds her beautiful body in the mirror
but still does not know herself. She resolves: "I will light candles
in front of the mirror. At midnight I will arise, naked. Inside
the moon of the mirror I will see my heart and will know my
destiny" (37). Life is comprehensible only by penetration of self.

Critics have isolated and interpreted other symbols in Godoy.
Moss is a symbol of softness; *dust* is indicative of age and passing
time; and the *soul* symbolizes the infinite. Their importance to
theme is minor and hence will not be detailed here.

From the foregoing interpretative study, it is apparent that
Godoy's symbols are man centered. Eyes, light, roots, the ox,
wine, and the mirror all symbolize aspects of humanity. The
symbols of ashes and sky are temporal expressions; Godoy relies
only slightly upon religious and classical symbolism. The majority of his symbols are original; meaning springs from recurrence in the work itself more than from outside sources. The
interconnection of iterative symbols raises literature from the
realms of here and today to a plane of imperishable, universal
value.[15]

IV   *Point of View: The Narrator Creates a World*

A further principle of Godoy's poetic Neo-Realism relates
to the type of narrator created by the author. In Godoy narrators
are usually complex and subjective and hence must be dealt
with individually. *Angurrientos* is told by an omniscient narrator
who does not appear directly in the story. He reports events
from an external viewpoint, beyond the novel's sphere of action.
He is close to his narrated universe, however, and is able to
paint intimate images—confidential smells, faint sounds, precise
tastes. His position varies between editorial and neutral omniscience:[16] he occasionally comments openly on attitudes or
actions, but he usually reports them without intrusive remark.
Narration is in the third person, usually in the past tense, except
in the case of poetic description, which is atemporalized by
omission of verbs. Narrative comment, introducing and accompanying dialogue, is normally in the past tense, too; however,

occasional shifts occur, giving a sudden closeness (or distance) to the moment of dialogue.

On numerous occasions, the all-powerful narrator of this novel permits one of his created beings to assume, temporarily, the role of narrator. Each one relates a short story within the novel, which may be compared to intercalated stories in such Spanish authors as Cervantes, Mateo Alemán, and Unamuno. The first two examples are stories of raising and fighting cocks (90-93). The other three, "Se ahogaron todos los piojos" (135-43), "El roto en el cenizo" (171-76), and the "Facico, Facica" popular story (194-98), are told by a novelistic character, rather than the narrator. The dangers of shifting from the omniscient narrator level to the character-narrator level are overcome in an introduction made by the original narrator: "Whenever sergeant began slipping over the cliff of drink into complete stupor, he *customarily related*, to anyone who would listen, 'El roto en el cenizo,'" my italics. Or, the omniscient narrator may state: "'We were all despairing,' *narrated Pedro*, beginning his story ..." my italics (170-71). By introducing the stories with "he customarily related" or "narrated Pedro...," the all-powerful narrator asserts himself over the new storyteller. As the character unfolds his tale, the reader knows that the original narrator will eventually return to carry the plot. The example shows a narrator so familiar with his character as to know Don Pedro's inclinations each time he gets drunk; the reader senses that the narration can be restored at any moment. With this type of control and smooth transition, the shifting of narrators in no way endangers verisimilitude. It must be added that this is not a new technique but simple conformity to time-proven literary conventions.

The narrator of *La cifra solitaria* is of a distinct nature, an indication of Godoy's creative depth. The point of view is personal, internal, and dramatized. The narrator is both an observer and a participant of the created world. The "I" is a witness to the events in the lives of others. At times he assumes the role of "I-protagonist," especially toward the novel's end, but most often he is simply a beholder of the events that transpire around him.

As the plot commences, the reader assumes that he is being led by a child: "The crackling of charcoal resounded under my youthful bare feet" (17). However, the narration expresses compassion too profound and language too poetic for the mind of

a child. The true narrator finally appears and confesses: "Even
now, in my mature years, I know..." (26). He is an adult,
recalling vivid events of his childhood. Through a first-person
narrator, the emotional experiences of the night of San Juan
are dramatized, and the reader feels an intimacy not possible
in omniscient narration. The story is more credible when told
by an internal participant, especially by a convincing, unbeguiled
youth. Further benefit is realized in the duality of the narrator.
Though relating the story from a child's point of view, he retains
the advantages of his maturity and distance. His temporal limitations are not those of a young lad; he perceives his characters'
past and what they will become, even in a future which has
little to do with the novel's action. The narrator, although
intimate, knows all—past, present, future; his omniscience surpasses that of an "I-witness" child.

The narrator fully controls the direction of the story; he is
not carried along by its events or by autonomous characters.
After picturing the cruel treatment heaped upon Chocholla, he
declares: "But I want to tell you now about Serafín, that extraordinary being, Chocholla's husband" (53). He moves freely
in time and space, leaving a previous scene to follow a new
character. This rapid shift and narrative control again reveal
a mature narrator, free to manipulate his story. The original
storyteller, the child, is dramatized and participates in the action.
The older man is an undramatized nonparticipating raconteur
and may be viewed as the "implied author" if such a category
need be established.[17] It is he who truly directs the narrative
development, as well as the child's narration, since he is supposedly the boy grown to maturity.

A further characteristic of the narrator of this novel is a
tendency toward vagueness. As a child would be, he is often
slightly confused about the world he beholds. He is not certain
he heard a statement correctly; he may misinterpret a grown-up's
look. In short, there may be varied interpretations to all actions:
"She stared at me.... *Maybe* she understood my thoughts. *Perhaps* she did because in her look there was..." (53). "Above, on
the crest of the mountain, *or perhaps in my mind,* Golondrino
proceeded..." (106). The last example, particularly, points up
his purposeful ambiguity. The child narrator is not sure whether
he actually saw Golondrino walking above the mountain or if
he simply imagined it. This technique adds verisimilitude to

the story and allows the reader to make final decisions, participating in the novel.

Similar to the first novel, Godoy employs the technique of
the shifting narrator in *La cifra solitaria*. The shift is not as
obvious as that in *Angurrientos*; it is merely a switch from one
first-person narrator to another, instead of from the third to the
first person. Before the wake, Golondrino briefly narrates three
short animal stories (68-70), showing cruelty and cunning. Then,
after the horror-filled wake, the midwife of the village relates
a miraculous story of the Virgin Mary. Although fascinated by
the fable, the narrator still maintains control through a formal
introduction: "As Eudoxia sipped her tea, we gathered around
to hear her enchanting tale of Romoán" (87). She proceeds,
but the reader knows that the true narrator must soon return.

The narrative techniques in *Sangre de murciélago* are the
most complicated of all Godoy's prose. Analogous to his earlier
writings, he permits a minor character to briefly narrate an
experience (202-7), is able to see the future beyond the present
narrative moment (92, 93), talks with familiarity to the reader
(78), and occasionally interrupts to comment on dialogue (80,
160). But here the similarities cease.

The narrator is a dramatized and internal "I-participant,"
more closely involved in his world than any other narrator in
Godoy. His "our admiral," "our violinist," "our friend," and so
on, promote an intimacy and closeness in which the reader also
participates. Rather than first-person singular, the narration is
often first-person plural. The narrator thus conveys the presence
of a group rather than an individual; occasionally he even loses
his own identity in the assemblage. Though he mingles with
the alcoholics of the story and participates in the created world,
he nevertheless assumes an elevated position in relation to other
novelistic characters: "We—the intellectuals—had freed ourselves
from these treatments..." (18). He maintains this superior
position throughout the entire novel and shares his sententious
familiarity with the reader, who in turn aligns himself with
the narrator.

In reality, there are two distinct narrators in the novel. The
original narrator is the professor of child psychology; but he
shares the stage with the sculptor, Pedro Ordóñez. Ordóñez
narrates approximately 40 percent of the work. Throughout the
novel, the narration moves from professor to sculptor; each pre-

sents his own life story. If a single narrator were to relate his
own dramatic life in first person, then shift to third person in
telling Ordóñez' history, much of the force and convincing
power would be lost. In shifting narrators, Godoy achieves
intimacy and conviction but sacrifices the unity possible through
use of a single narrator.[18]

Change of narrator also creates a definite instability. The
reader is not always certain just who is speaking, or, if he is
informed, he may confuse the two characters. The confusion
is neither error nor oversight, however, but Godoy's purposeful
creation of unstable reality. Just as the created characters—
dipsomaniacs and drug addicts—live in two worlds or in a
confusion of both, so Juan Godoy mixes reality with fantasy,
one man with another, the novelistic world with the real world,
and so forth. This vision of an unstable reality opens when a
doctor praises Chilean products, stating: "I recall now, a toast
offered by Juan Godoy, an unknown Chilean writer" (56). The
mention of the author as a novelistic character, or as a part of
the novelistic world, is not new to Spanish letters. Cervantes,
Velázquez, Unamuno, and many others have used this technique
as one way of immortalizing themselves along with their creations. Two separate worlds blend. Juan Godoy never physically
appears in the novel, but his poetic toast is recited and is sufficient
to unite him with the created characters. Yet the all-wise reader
knows that a Juan Godoy actually exists in contemporary Chile
and that he is indeed an unknown writer. The effect is one of
purposeful confusion of distance.

A parallel to Unamuno's autonomous characters is noted when
the direction of the story is forcibly wrested from the narrator's
hands and taken over by Ordóñez. Unlike Godoy's other shifting
narrators, the first speaker no longer has control over the second.
The true narrator starts out: "It seems that I've forgotten to
tell of the life of my sculptor friend" (62). Ordóñez rudely
interrupts: "Dear friend, allow me to tell about myself. You know
that all who work in the plastic arts must at some time attempt
a self-portrait. Let your pen fall into my hands ..." (62). But
the narrator shows his omniscience and temporal superiority
over Ordóñez, with: "Now that I write this, Ordóñez belongs to
eternity where deeds are not staked out in a temporal line. And
he took the words from me" (62-3). In true Unamunesque fashion,
the freed character replies to the narrator, and then addresses

the reader: "It is to you, reader or listener, that I speak. Imagine, eager friend, a thin man, tall.... I killed myself underneath the wheels of a freight train, some months ago" (63). Not to be upstaged by the narrator, the independent character informs the reader of his own death. By so doing, he elevates himself above the narrator, who is trapped in the world of the novel. Ordóñez' vision is limitless, and he boasts of it. The effect of this battle between narrator and aspiring narrator is one of bewilderment and turmoil. The reader is not sure whom to believe; he must simply follow both storytellers until the conflict is resolved. No solution is achieved; Ordóñez and the narrator alternately vie for supremacy. Both are intimate and dramatic; they accomplish the already mentioned ends of first-person narration. At the novel's conclusion, the original narrator is finally able to assert himself and stabilize reality by allowing the reader to witness Ordóñez' death (240).

Four of Godoy's short stories are told with a dramatized "I-protagonist." Three of these are adults, one is a young boy. The child's story, "El ramal, o el canario bombero," is the most artistic and faithfully conforms to the limits of childhood experience and psychology. "Un inspector de sanidad...." presents the curious case of a short story based almost exclusively on dialogue. The dramatized narrator has little to do but order the dialogue, until one of the speakers quiets the others and finishes the narration himself; thus, the narrator loses his primacy.

Two of the stories are related from a non-dramatic, external point of view. The narrators do not enter into their world. "Sombras" is an odd mixture of internal and external, first- and third-person narration. The events that set the background for the story are told by a distant but compassionate narrator. At first he remains separate from his world; but when he begins the action of the story, he switches to an intimate first-person account. Later he distances himself again, only to regain first-person involvement for the final dramatic scene. The blending of the two processes is done so well that the reader reaps the advantages of both techniques, without accompanying disadvantages.

DRAMATIZED NARRATORS. In the majority, Godoy's narrators are dramatized and participate in the novelistic action. Only in his first novel and one short story ("El profesor y unos pelusas") does he rely on an omniscient narrator throughout.

And even in these two works the narrator is close to his world, free to enter with editorial comment, value judgment, and the like. The narrators Godoy creates actively participate in life and possess follies and foibles like all the other characters. Stories are told from an internal rather than from an external point of view.

In the use of internal viewpoint Godoy gains several narrative advantages. When the tale is strange or supernatural, an experience is more convincingly told by a narrator who has actually participated in the action. Such is the case in the death of the pups, Satan's defeat, and Golondrino's transformation in *La cifra solitaria*. The "I" promotes intimacy; he tells his tale from the heart. From this intimacy the story gains vividness. Also aided by a dramatized, first-person narration is the coherence and unity which a participant in the novelistic world can bring to the plot.

In the short stories Godoy's dramatized narrators are "I" as a protagonist, but in the novels the "I" is alternately protagonist and witness. Loncho, the child of the second novel, has certain problems of his own which occasionally make him the central figure, but he is generally merely observer to that which happens around him. Even the adult narrator of *Sangre de murciélago* frequently leaves the center stage and becomes an observer of others' lives.

SHIFTING NARRATORS. Only in three of his short stories is Godoy content to leave the narrative reins in the hands of a single story-teller. In each of his other works, the original narrator allows incidental characters to relate a story; they contribute a multiple viewpoint. Their narration consists of an intercalated story, usually of popular origin, and contributes a poetic, folkloric tone rather than an advancement of plot. The transition between storytellers is handled smoothly, with the original narrator maintaining ultimate control.

Both classes of narrators are reliable, acting in accordance with the norms of the work.[19] The shifting does not weaken the narration but diversifies and adds credence to it.

NARRATIVE DISTANCE. Dramatized and intimate, Godoy's narrators are close to the world they describe. They make judgments, talk with others, perceive images with all their senses, refer to characters in intimate terms, and generally remain near the created realms of the novelistic world. Godoy utilizes a fascinating method to indicate the proximity of the narrator. It may be called the "peephole technique." It is the manner in which the boy Loncho learns of the world: "There, in the neighboring room, lived Serafín the butcher and his wife Chocholla. A crack in the scaly wall threw out a beam of light. This peephole opened my eyes and showed me many things about the intimate life of those miserable beings" (*La cifra solitaria*, 17). Through his wall Loncho perceives most of the events which he organizes and narrates. Naturally his world is not confined to the limited perspective of one small hole; he occasionally leaves the house, but the major narrative action occurs as he peers at his neighbors.

Even the more omniscient narrator of *Angurrientos* occasionally resorts to the same technique, revealing his contiguous position: "Through the slits in the wall, knives of light cut the darkness" (162). "The old man who waited on the sergeant's table peered through a hole, hidden in the wall, at the bar next door..." (177).

Fortunately, the narrator's closeness to his created world does not distance him from his readers. In all the novels and two of the short stories the narrator pauses, leaving the narrative thread, to talk to the reader. This kind of second-person narration promotes a confidence and friendly relationship between narrator and reader, bringing the reader closer to the novelistic world and allowing him the same viewpoint as the narrator.

In summary, Godoy takes full advantage of available techniques to strengthen his story. The narrators, in each case, add to, rather than detract from, the content. Each is appropriate to the subject matter, inventing just the right illusion for the story. Godoy's narrators create a world in which they are free to enter or disappear at will. They may not behave according to the rules of an esthetic technician, but they do follow the norms of the work itself—all that can be required of an author.

V *Characterization*

The problem of how an author creates his characters is of lasting concern to the critic and reader; they must be made live and real. In Godoy, physical appearance and traits are of little importance. It is the soul of man that he characterizes in detail, a soul he considers poetic. Hence, characterization is another of the many elements of poetic narration in prose. Godoy pursues the unchanging internal man and his spiritual makeup rather than physical appearances. Characterization is an opening of inner realities. Thoughts, fears, plans, desires, and motives are exposed to the reader by an all-seeing narrator who respects no secrets. This technique is most effective in describing developing, dynamic character. But it is used with all of Godoy's creations: "Edmundo wanted to discover *his* truth, understand it at any cost. He knew the painful anguish of existence.... Would he be nothing more than mediocre? None of his friends were mediocre..." (*Angurrientos*, 43).

Another clue to the understanding of man's inner soul is his speech. Hence the dialogue of Godoy's novels becomes an important key to character. The narrator simply gives free rein to the loquacious actors, who enjoy philosophizing and baring their souls. The short stories contain little dialogue, but the novels are replete with it. Each successive novel brings increased dialogue, until in *Sangre de murciélago* and *El impedido* conversation far surpasses narration. A wise critic observes that man in this novel "functions as an 'agonist,' in Unamuno fashion."[20] Like Unamuno's agonists or agonic characters, Godoy's characters are permitted to create themselves as they discourse. In conflict with himself, the literary figure must talk to reveal his soul. As he effects dialogue with others, his life of doubt and self-annihilation is bared, and he becomes more aware of self. He is a man without a defined philosophy of life, a man who attempts to create something concrete through dialogue. The technique is used to such an extent in the first hundred pages of *Sangre de murciélago* that the reader yearns for action and less conversation. The other novels achieve a greater balance between dialogue and narration. Dialogue in Godoy does not serve exclusively to further characterization, as might be imagined; it often functions to dramatize action.

To expose man's inner life, Godoy's narrators make use of all available methods: they penetrate the character's soul, allow him to dialogue with other characters, tune in on his interior monologue, reveal his most intimate dreams, and interpret his subconscious.

As a movement deeply rooted in lyric expression, it is logical that Angurrientism would produce poetic characters. Some are realistic commoners, but many are poetic, more akin to fantasy than iniquitous flesh. This is especially true of the first two novels. Some disconcerted critics see only disharmony in mixing terrestrial and fantastic personages.[21] But as part of a movement designed to penetrate the soul of the Chilean, Godoy is perfectly justified in mixing fantasy with reality; he finds in his subjects just such polarity, similarly and harmoniously blended. The poor, common man's life is so deeply ingrained with folklore and popular legends that characters from these sources become as real to him as do his contemporaries. This mingling of characters from life and legend greatly enhances the universal nature of the poor Chilean.

The lyric makeup of Godoy's characters evolves through his early novels to the short stories and last novel. The characters move from the poetic to the grotesque. From the "El Cenizo," "Pistolas," Golondrino, and Doña Eudoxia of the early years, deforming changes occur, producing characters just as fantastic, but with an added note of absurdity. The corpulent, ludicrous innkeeper Amelia, and the pock-marked, blind beggar of "The Professor...," the inflated government official, the character "Bat's Blood," and many other loquacious beings are characterized by their absurdity. Neither realistic nor poetic characterizations, they may be best described as "esperpentic," from Valle-Inclán.

In review, Godoy's novelistic figures fall into three types of characters: realistic, poetic, and "esperpentic." Any two of the three may combine in the same world, but rarely are all three united. The early works tend toward poetic and realistic characters; the latter blend realistic with "esperpentic." This admixture causes no confusion or esthetic weakening; Godoy's created world admits all types. If his works were pure social documents, unrealistic figures would weaken the unity, and "esperpentic" characters would destroy it. But, as has already been noted, Godoy takes pains to integrate poetry and nonlogical association. The result is the harmonious coexistence of poetic, absurd, and realistic characters.

Few of Godoy's characters are sufficiently dynamic to effect changes in their lives. Changing figures are extremely difficult to characterize. Only Edmundo and Wanda of *Angurrientos* and the boy narrators in *La cifra solitaria* and "El ramal" experience significant transition. Their changes are consistent with their character: each has the intrinsic capacity for change; they are motivated by circumstances; and ample time is allowed for the change. Edmundo's transition is minor; he descends from an inquisitive search for "his truth," to resignation to life's inconsistencies. He abandons his search and escapes anxiety through drink. Wanda, on the other hand, is an ascending character, turning from passive acceptance of her sad life to determined action. The youth of the second novel has only a few hours in which to effect a change; his only transition is caused by a single moving experience, which leaves a deep impression and gives rise to new determination. The most tender and probably the most convincing change takes place in the young narrator of "The Whip." Rarely does significant change occur in a short story, but through one anguished experience, Godoy masterfully demonstrates growth from playful childhood to compassionate manhood.

Godoy's developing characters convince the reader of their reality. They change in verisimilar ways, consistent with their previous life. It was undoubtedly these few nonstatic figures which inspired Marta Brunet's eulogistic statement that Godoy has created "eternal novelistic characters in Chilean literature."[22]

A major advance over Criollism is the deeper, more internal characterization in the works of the generation of 1938. Godoy devotes chapters and, at times, an entire novel, to establishing the nature and makeup of a character. No major figure is so simple that a single presentation suffices. Godoy's concern is with the inner man, rarely with outward appearances. Description of clothing, for example, is completely absent from his works. Clothes are easily changed; inner realities are not. Through direct report by the narrator, free dialogue, interior monologue, dreams, and secret ambitions, the reader is privileged to know the spiritual essence of Godoy's characters.

Godoy does not belabor characterization; he merely outlines and suggests enough to identify and humanize his figures. His works do not create towering heroes. Lasting impressions arise not from individual characters but from the entire created world. In this respect, his men and women approach agonic, Unamunesque proportions, rather than the protagonic, hero types of earlier centuries.

In the delineation of "flat" and "round," major and minor, realistic and poetic characters, Godoy always moves from physical to spiritual detail. Some of his characters are typed by their physical appearance, but even these possess a spiritual dimension which corroborates the external. While many are "static" and nondeveloping, none of Godoy's characters is lifeless; all overflow with an abundance of life, a "vital desire for life."

VI *Structure and the Problem of Novelistic Form*

Godoy's most innovative contribution to Chilean prose is the creation of new possibilities in novelistic form. Criollism depended upon a cause-and-effect relationship to establish orderly temporal progression. Event B followed as a logical consequence of event A, and the inevitable finale was determined by all that preceded it. Time and space were incidental to an episodic plot. Godoy was one of the first to introduce revolutionary modifications to Criollist patterns. So radical are many of his changes, especially those dealing with narrative form, that many refuse to acknowledge his works as novels.[23] However, his works *do* maintain the essentials of the novel: plot, character, problem, and theme. In Chile most critics highly defend and heartily welcome the new techniques employed in Godoy's prose: "There's nothing wrong with calling this type of prose [*La cifra solitaria*] a novel. Those who sidestep the term and use such words as 'scene,' 'stamp,' or 'memorial,' are hardly sincere or else do not realize that the novel changes; it is a living genre."[24] The inspiring Domingo Melfi recognizes the worth of Godoy's writings and has no hesitation in calling *Angurrientos* a novel: "a complex novel, not conforming to classical principles of the genre, but wrought with the same vital disunity with which life is woven...."[25]

STRUCTURE. Godoy's novels are divided into parts and chapters. Each of the first two novels contains two parts; *Sangre de murciélago* three; *El impedido* is a short novel. The purpose of the divisions is traditional—to allow for a change in time or space. In *Angurrientos* at least eight weeks elapse between the first and second parts, an interval necessary for one of the major characters to fall gravely ill. The division of *La sifra solitaria* occurs when shift of both time and place are necessary; the child narrator has been recalling a fishing experience with Golondrino, prior to the dramatic present moment of the original narration. The second part takes him back to his home and to the main thread of the story. The three parts of *Sangre de murciélago* likewise indicate some important change of time, space, or attitude.

Going one division lower, each part is organized into chapters, once again a traditional grouping. On this level the reader senses Godoy's disparity with previous writers. Some chapters are drawn out to fifty or more pages; others are abbreviated to a single page. Hence, the chapter ceases to be an isolatable, unified body. One chapter may recount many events; another may contain virtually no action of significance. Obviously, then, action is not the criterion for Godoy's chapter divisions. The chapter is a thematic unit, expressing a given concept about man. It need not further the narrative action but must convey a unified, man-centered theme. The chapters of the second novel, especially, are worded so that each title conveys a philosophical idea about man: "A Tiny Light Is Filled with Fear," "Horrible Sensations of Breath," "The Dog Licked His Tears," "The Perforated Nut." This tendency to develop chapters as thematic, contemplative units, rather than as divisions of action has disconcerted many readers who expect traditional structure. Though seemingly erratic, Godoy's structure actually strengthens his novel, through emphasizing intellectual approximation rather than plot involvement.

Setting apart an even smaller structural division is Godoy's use of three astericks (***) to separate two parts of the same chapter. Such divisions occur in each of Godoy's novels and in four short stories. They are subdivisions of the chapter and indicate either (1) a minor shift in time or space (first quote below) or (2) a shift from narrative description to poetic contemplation of nature (second quote).

(1) "Old Pistols," caught up in her past, recalled that Encarnation Catalán laughed like a hawk at her husband.

*   *   *

The next morning, as usual .... (*Angurrientos,* 164)

(2) There was just one remaining, the six o'clock bus.

*   *   *

That afternoon the mountains wrapped themselves in tenuous clouds and shadows of clouds.... And the tint of the sun between the clouds at evening was an autumn leaf descending gently from the sky.

*   *   *

On the other side of Puente Alto a couple approached. (*Sangre de murciélago,* 156)

These divisions within the chapter allow the narrator great freedom of expression. He is not bound by temporal limitations of the narrative moment and may jump forward a day or move to an entirely different location. The cohesiveness of the chapter is achieved not through consistency of action, time, or space but through unity of theme. With such emancipation, the narrator is able to introduce any event or idea which contributes to thematic harmony.

FLEXIBILITY OF FORM. The prose of this innovative novelist does not conform to or abide by previous narrative patterns. Formal structure is too stiff for Godoy's heterogeneous themes. Hence, new techniques must be applied to novelistic structure. Godoy's flexibility expands the possibilities of the created world. Progression of the narrative is usually intuitive, shunning rational order. Intuitive progression functions to bring the disorder, irrationality, and variegated experiences of life to the realm of the novel. Man perceives his surroundings irrationally; a novel, the author contends, must be sufficiently pliable to reproduce the same distortion. Though any ordered unity may be destroyed, the form of the novel coincides with expression: life is disordered and irrational; so is novelistic form. "Godoy has attempted to express the vital movement of life, without geometrical order of plot, without the neatly-worked denouement, with the valiant conquering hero. . . . His is a dynamic prose."[26] There is a spontaneity in Godoy's narration rarely found in novelistic creation. As in real life, characters are briefly introduced and quickly pass, leaving scarcely a trace on the world. Memories mix with immediate experience. Urgencies demand an abrupt shift of attention. All this is done to reproduce life as the narrator sees it—disarranged, tragic, and chaotic.

INTERCALATION. In each of the author's novels and in two short stories poetry and song are intercalated into the narration. This in itself exemplifies flexibility of structure; but intercalation serves other purposes. In *Angurrientos* twenty-two popular songs or poems add rhythm, poetry, and vernacular tone to the narration. Nineteen of these intercalated poems are of popular origin—*tonadas, cuecas,* and old picaresque songs. Musical instruments are frequently humanized and normally accompany the character who sings the popular song. Godoy has gathered this folkloric element from all parts and times of Chile. Two of the songs have their origin in the folklore of the black man, who

has long since disappeared from Chile. Some date to colonial
times (88, 140). Many speak of love and sadness; most contain
some note of humor or irony. Several are sung as counterpoints:
one figure starts the verse, a second answers with succeeding
lines. They are precisely the songs and ditties one would hear
in a bar or in a casual conversation with a poetic friend. Their
inclusion in Godoy's prose lends a true flavor of the Chilean soul.

Mixed with these nineteen popular ballads are examples of
more cultured, belabored poetry: there is one quote from a
Golden Age poet and two from Godoy's own poetic expressions
(109, 123). In the first one, Godoy breaks up a popular Spanish
expression ("You can't expect pears from the elm tree"), adds
an idea from a fable of Aesop, and creates a poem which suc-
cintly expresses the theme of the chapter: "A mass of green
pears!/ Fox of the grapes!/ Elm, elm, elm!" The second is a
feigned prayer, combining religious and erotic elements.

Only two examples of popular verse appear in the second
novel, each adding to folkloric expression. In *Sangre de murciélago*
six poems or songs are employed: four popular ballads (one
from Mexico), a poem of Baudelaire, and a poetic toast by Godoy.

The purposes of Godoy's intercalated poetry are multiple.
By breaking up the normal rhythm of the prose sentence, poetic
swing is created. To a Chilean, familiar with the *tonadas* and
words that accompany this national dance, the poetry evokes
intimacy and may even move the reader to sing or hum the
melody. But popular appeal is not the only value; the words
of the song or poem harmonize with the content of the chapter.
The *tonada* is often a concise poetic summary of present or
preceding action. As such, it simulates the function of the
chorus in a Greek drama. While each song or verse conveys
its own message, it also expresses the mood of the entire narrative.
It is not merely an appendage but an indispensable part of
the prose:

> I'm a poor lost bird,
> Wandering alone,
> In unhappy branches,
> Seeking a home.
> I begin my flight,
> But my wings betray me;
> Oh, I cannot fly!   (128)

Interspersed throughout each novel are one or more tales which may be considered true short stories. Each has a unity of its own, independent of the main narration, yet each contributes to the narration. Examples from *Angurrientos* are: "Cock Fighting" (61-82), "All the Lice Drowned" (135-43); "The Stolen Pig" (154-65), "The Ash-colored Cock" (171-76), "The Facico/Facica Story" (194-98), and "The Kidnapping of Betty Peel" (215-18). *La cifra solitaria* contains "The Story of Romoán" (87-91). *Sangre de murciélago* has three such stories: "The Bat-blood Cure" (77-89), "Buzzard" (112-16), and "Little Mother" (201-7).

The first novel is the most varied; six short stories enrich the narration. Of the six, only the Facico/Facica story seems somewhat extraneous being removed in time from the rest of the action. The other five stories, though not directly involved in the plot, intensify the theme by depicting scenes similar to those of the novelistic sphere; thus, they amplify the author's created world. While intercalated stories may detract from plot harmony, they strengthen thematic unity. "Cock Fighting" intensifies the theme by presenting the poor man's whirlwind involvement in cockfighting. A single event, within the plot, could not expose the myriad facets of psychological and physical involvement revealed by this intensified short story. "The Ash-colored Cock" demonstrates the fantasy and supernatural belief that are part of the common man's life. The inclusion of fantasy in the main thread of the plot would have brought critical cries of unbelief and inverisimilitude. As an intercalated story it does not detract from plausibility. "All the Lice Drowned" is so complete within itself that it appeared as a short story in Guzmán's 1941 anthology and in Godoy's 1952 collection, under the new title, "Herminia Gets Revenge." While it can stand alone, its chief purpose is to establish the character of its narrator, Horacio.

Unlike the above, the story of Romoán from the second novel does not occur in the same sphere as the rest of the novel. Its function, like the "Twelve Magic Words" that immediately precedes it, is both folkloric and mythical. It exploits the popular element, likely to be found at a death wake. At the same time its jovial, happy tone juxtaposes the morbose, frightening encounter with the devil in the previous chapter.

The first short story of the third novel, "The Bat-blood Cure," is necessary to explain the title of the novel. It relates closely to the world of the novel, explaining the behavior of one of the minor characters. The other two stories are necessary to characterize the two narrators.

ACTIVE AND CONTEMPLATIVE NARRATION: THE "STAMP". Godoy's prose is so structured that there is a continual oscillation between action and contemplation. The narrator commences, relating an event in a character's life. Suddenly this active narration shifts to contemplative, lyric description, while the narrator revels in beauty. After a brief poetic pause, he returns to the action, only to be distracted again by some exquisite scene from nature. Hence there is a pattern established: action-contemplation-action-contemplation, and so on. This oscillation characterizes all of Godoy's prose, even the short stories. It is as if the narrator simply cannot relate action without expressing his ecstasy over the beautiful environs. Lyric expression is sometimes separated from the active narration by the three astericks mentioned earlier but often springs forth without any structural break. Within "In the Bellies of Wine," a chapter of Godoy's first novel, the narration fluctuates nine times between contemplation and action. The first paragraph is lyric. No human figure appears until the final words of the last sentence—the misty blue light illuminates the room, the objects in the room, and finally, "the sleeping faces." The following paragraph is active narration: "Sergeant Ovalle snored, seated in the chair...." But the narrator finds the surroundings more appealing than the human subject, and the succeeding paragraph returns to lyric contemplation: "The blue air, that surrounded and penetrated the substance of waking things, sprinkled the bird's song and her dew trickled down the sticky red abdomen of the figs. Underneath the soft, humid reeds the little streamlets filled with living, self-conscious light, sang their melody." Misty morning, with all her life, replaces action. No human is visible; all is natural beauty.

In the following paragraph the narrator returns to active description: "Ovalle yawned; rubbed his eyes...." The next six paragraphs are active description, dealing with Ovalle, his thoughts, and his frustrations. The final sentence concludes: "And he silently slipped into the street, in search of his own life and death." The spatial transition from the interior of the house to the street outside is sufficient for a three-asterick break. In the following paragraph, the narrator again leaves Ovalle and proceeds to lyricize the grace of the natural world: "In reality, a burst of gold flooded the valley, fleshy with ripe grapes...." A whole paragraph of poetic description follows. A three-asterick break precedes another brief return to active narration: "Sergeant Ovalle entered Salto Lane...." But the narrator, in the next sentence, again digresses to lyric observation: "Before his eyes a field of grapes, melons, and fruits. The green of carrot tops. Corn...." And throughout the entire paragraph his portrayal of trees, fruits, streamlets, and shadows continues. This lyric representation then leads him back to his main action. As Ovalle walks along, nature becomes a part of him, and his progress is slowed by his involvement in the natural world. The only real physical action of the chapter is his walk to the bar. Once inside, the final paragraph again is lyric: "Sipping his soup, Ovalle contemplated the straw-colored hills whose stomach sported the deep scar of the stone quarry. Foothills cultivated in patches, and above, a dress of thorns and pine."

The chapter selected for analysis is not unique; most of *Angurrientos* is structured similarly. The same creative technique is evident in all of Godoy's works, including the short stories, where such a technique is somewhat surprising (*La cifra solitaria,* 9-16; "El gato de la maestranza," 28-31; "El profesor," 39-44; "El ramal," 115-17; *Sangre de murciélago,* 15-17).

A trinary pattern in the narration is established: lyric expression-active description-lyric expression. A chapter frequently opens with a poeticized scene which establishes the mood. Then action erupts onto the scene, the events of the story are climaxed, and action once again gives way to contemplation. The pattern creates the effect, in prose, of an act from a tense drama. As the curtain is raised, only the setting is perceived. After moments of viewing the beautiful backdrop, actors appear, perform their roles, and disappear, leaving the viewer to bask in the quiet, motionless panorama once again. The same effect is achieved in narrative prose, where the reader finishes a chapter enthralled by the lyric moment rather than by the plot or story. It must be recognized that Godoy modifies and varies this trinary pattern; if he did not, his prose would be monotonous and facile. A chapter may commence with active narration, move to contemplation, and finish with action. Or it may only go through the first two steps. Most common, however, is the three-part, lyric-active-lyric pattern.

Moments of lyric description create the most characteristic mark of Godoy's prose—the "stamp"—a scene in which lyric and contemplative elements predominate over action. Human beings are usually absent, and movement is minimal. Description, rather than direct, becomes metaphoric. Thus, Godoy is a landscape painter as well as a novelist; he is a Van Gogh in letters. While the fluctuation between active and lyric narration creates the sensation of drama, the "stamp" has the impact of an impressionistic painting. It pictures natural surroundings, sky, earth, trees, birds, cultivated fields, and so forth:

A cold sun on the summit snows, a diffused sky. The white rigging of the frost, hardened spider webs. . . . Nude grape arbors, with petticoats of putrid gold, above the puddles, above the dew, livid grass. (*Angurrientos*, 154)

In the black sky the moon extended her cold silver-blue foliage. She flooded the mountain, the ravines, the river. The fig tree skated down the greenish frost. (*La cifra solitaria*, 100)

It is the hour when streets turn their pale face to the dawn. A drizzle wraps the city in gloomy nets. It caps houses, pavement, tired faces, with a patina of opaque dirty glass. Luminous rays of blood, blue, pink, yellow, flee through the street. (*El gato de la maestranza*, 19)

The frequent poetic use of these "stamps" has occasioned comparison of Godoy with Gabriel Miró. But Miró's "stamps" are static and are often an end in themselves; little, if any, action occurs in the immovable sketches. They are fixed prints rather than visions of a living world. The author is not personally close to the world of his characters.[27] Beautiful for the sake of beauty, Godoy's "stamps" do possess some elements of static narration, such as verbal ellipses, but for the most part they are lively, vital representations of the world. Humanized nature imparts life to the scene: grapevines are sensuous women in golden petticoats; city streets pulsate with the lifeblood of their neon signs; mountains are clothed with velvet trees. These scenes are not static; man enters and becomes a part of the natural world. The mingling of man and nature brings new life to the setting. Sergeant Ovalle steps out of his house, and the beauty of the scene compels him to participate with nature. Godoy's "stamps" are made dynamic by the movement that takes place within them. The major backdrop may not change radically, but there is always a shaft of light, a shadow, a gurgling stream, or a bird in song to enliven the landscape. And finally, it is man and his activity—his "vital desire for life"—that bestows the ultimate spark of vitality. Godoy is not merely a Chilean Miró.

"Stamps" aid in the creation of poetic prose. Prose is linked to the plastic arts, particularly to painting. Each scene is like a picture, perceived instantaneously. Díaz-Plaja employs the term "little vision" and compares its effect to that of impressionistic painting.[28]

NARRATIVE PROGRESSION—CONCENTRIC TECHNIQUE. Structural development of Criollist works is generally horizontal. That is, the action evolves in an organized manner from point A, to B, to C, to conclusion, D. The chronological ordering of time is logical and presents no difficulty for the reader. In short, the narrative progresses on a horizontal, organized plane. Narrative development is a straight line.

Godoy's prose, on the other hand, shuns facile, flat development in favor of uneven, seemingly disordered, narration. Rather than begin at point A and progress in order to conclusion D, the novel may open in the middle of an event, advance to a given point, go back to an as-yet-unmentioned beginning, and then conclude. Or, it may begin with the first chronological event, suffer repeated interruptions, and return to the mainstream of the action for conclusion. Narrative progression is concentric rather than horizontal. In all cases, there is a common center around which the events of the plot revolve. Godoy's goal, and that of the whole generation, was a deeper penetration of man's psyche. To accomplish this exacting objective, Godoy devised the system of placing a man in the center of the narration. Around the central figure revolve his past and present, his friends and foes, his fancies and failures, bestowing him with depth and humanity. The reader perceives more than physical appearance; the soul is bared, revealing an anguished being rather than a mere novelistic caricature. An examination of narrative progression in each of Godoy's three main works reveals his concentric design.

The initial scene in *Angurrientos* is a "stamp," a vision of poverty and sorrow on the outskirts of Santiago. The entire novel is structured around this scene. The reader is never allowed to leave the filth and struggle of life once he enters; each of the eight scenes in the novel is set within the squalor of the *barrio*. Each serves more deeply to penetrate the unhappy reality of man in misery. Godoy's "minute nook" is the center

of his novelistic world and gives unity to the seemingly disjointed sections. Individual chapters add depth to that world;
they are the interlocking segments of concentric pattern, fortify-
ing the common center.

One character, Edmundo, juts into prominence in this negative world, appearing more often than any other. He endures,
from his idealistic beginnings, to conformity and pessimism at
the end. The narration returns repeatedly to follow Edmundo's
quest, which is woven through the entire novel before being
resolved. Though Edmundo is not present in each scene, it is
his search for meaning in life which lends cohesion to the novel.
Thus, Edmundo becomes the human center of the narrative
action, and many events of the novel are included simply because they reveal the deep anguish of his soul. He is the concentric midpoint for the novel.

Edmundo relates in some way to each of the major characters
of the work. He is Wanda's boyfriend, Don Amaranto's scribe,
Augusto's rival and sometime friend, and, toward the novel's
conclusion, a drinking companion to El Cojín, Rey Humberto,
Anabalón, and Fraile Horacio. While each of these characters
dominates the narrative action for a brief period, the story
always returns to anguished Edmundo. He performs no heroic
feat in the novelistic world; he is only searching. Each time the
camera switches from the more active, Angurrientist characters to pick up Edmundo, he is caught in questioning contemplation. In this way, the young student's soul is exposed to the
reader, whereas only the actions of other characters are portrayed. Each time Edmundo appears, or is mentioned, more of
his innermost ambitions are revealed.

The first reference to him streams from Wanda's memory. But
not until Wanda has completed her affairs does Edmundo appear
in person. On this occasion, Amaranto attempts to force Edmundo into the confessional, but the self-respecting youth cannot
acknowledge his sins before the unctuous priest. Shortly, the
reader understands that Edmundo is seeking "his truth"—a
meaning in life (41). On two occasions Edmundo expresses his
quandary (43, 52). Various other actors and actions intervene,
but the narrator returns again and again to Edmundo. After
an absence of three chapters, the narrator finds him again, still
in the time and the place he had been left: "Edmundo had

brought about his shipwreck, his truth. And since it was his own truth, he found it very strange" (101).

After this sorry discovery, Edmundo disappears from the narrative scene while Ovalle, Pistolas, Amaranto, and Wanda display and explain their mottled souls. Slightly drunk, the young student turns up at the deathbed of Ovalle (220). He is not heard from again until the problems of all the other characters have been resolved. After everyone else leaves the stage, Edmundo emerges from a bar, "drunk, broken in spirit, lacking all desire and will to continue" (248). Losing his will, he conforms to his infelicitous surroundings. The.tragedy of his conformity is heightened by concentric narration. The narrator's frequent return to the student's disconsolate life places Edmundo at the center of the stage. Narrative progression is inward, toward Edmundo, rather than a horizontal examination of a wide social segment.

A further example of concentric narration in the novel is the repetition of the cockfighting theme, thoroughly interwoven through the life of each character. No real progress takes place in the cockfighting scenes; the first is no different from any other. Each fight is so similar, in fact, that the narrator even repeats his own words in recalling two contests (80, 245). Consequently, little horizontal progression is registered, but intense penetration of one point occurs.

In the first part of *La cifra solitaria* concentric narration is a problem of time. A fluctuation between indefinite past events and the tense circumstances of Chocolla's beating, creates a narrative world with a common center, one in which past participates freely in the present. The narrator begins in an indefinite past time. The second chapter is the present, the Night of San Juan. Chapter 3 begins on the same night but soon dissolves to an unspecified time in the boy's memory, as he recalls ageless Golondrino. The following two chapters are set in the same vague past. Then, in typical Godoyan style, the narrator returns to the events of the mystical night. His departure from what could have been chronological, horizontal progression after the second chapter, deepens the meaning of the semireligious events that follow. The story proceeds in normal order until the intervention of Doña Eudoxia's story, after which the narration is definitely not chronologically ordered; reflective pauses arise which demand a return to the novel's common center, the Night of San Juan.

The narrative progression in *Sangre de murciélago* is Godoy's most complex. As in the second novel, the problem is chiefly one of temporal shift. The novel exposes the spiritual and moral descent in the life of an alcoholic. Merely observing the actions of these men over a brief period of time could not adequately suggest hidden reaches of their world. To give fuller meaning, the narrator places each character in situations where his past can be unveiled. A clear, bright morning, for example, evokes childhood memories for Ordóñez; the narrator's accounting of his own history moves Ordóñez to do likewise. Conversations with fellow inmates also allow for recollection and explanation of the past. Hence, narrative progression is an oscillation from the immediate reality of the institution to the individual lives of the alcoholics before commitment.

There are fourteen shifts, all of which add meaning to the present. Through fluctuation between past and present time, Godoy achieves a gradual unfolding of the alcoholic mind. Had progress been purely chronological or included only one penetrating trip into the past, the characters would lack depth and convincing vitality. Godoy's concentric design, with frequent return to the past, builds plausibility; the present, living character, rather than past life and deeds, is established as paramount. Though only eight months actually pass in the novel, the entire lives of two men are reviewed. Unlike the orderly progression of the Criollists, Godoy's techniques allow him more fully to discern and interpret the essence of man.[29]

DREAM. The narrative sequence in Godoy's final novel is diversified by eight dreams. In his earlier works, dreams occur infrequently, are usually short, and can be readily understood. Those of *Sangre de murciélago* are lengthy and involved. They are: The Missing Liver (69), The Disintegrating Body (71), The Grapevine and the Sensuous Woman (98), The Otter and the Horse (148), The Headless, Rubber People (191), The Honey and the Flower (229), The Dead Soldier (230), and The Pirate/Soldier Battle (230). Delusion, deception, disintegration, and mutilation—the subjects of these dreams—are studied in the chapter on man. The effect of the dreams on structure is foremost here. Like intercalated incidents, they interrupt the flow of the narrative. Also like Godoy's intercalated short stories, they complement theme. Ordóñez' dream of the dead otter coming to life (148) and cruelly masticating the testicles of a horse is immediately mirrored in Cona's aggression and possessive attitude toward the sculptor (152).

The ironical highlight of the novel is the tragicomic dream of the missing liver. Overly concerned with the function of this organ, Ordóñez awakes one morning and reaches for his habitual bottle. Unable to find it, "I sunk my hand in my right side, in the hole where my liver should be, and I didn't find it." Desperate, he discovers the liver on the table wrapped in newsprint, but he is assured by a loving wife that if he swallows it whole, it will return to its proper place (70-71). This humorous reverie contrasts sharply with the solemn controversy over alcoholism which it has interrupted. It points up a haunting concern for the problem discussed. Dreams provide a valuable tool to the author in enriching content and in strengthening the structure of the novel.

RHYTHM. The major effect of the techniques studied above is rhythmic. They alter narrative rhythm from the normal pattern of straightforward description to the peculiarities of poetic prose. Irregular rhythm characterizes all of Godoy's prose. The several intercalated stories break the flow of narration, allowing the reader to pause and reflect. They do not, however, permit complete departure from the novelistic world, since their themes are consistent with the theme of the novel. But they do create a lapse in the novel's narrative events. As such, they provide intermittent rests for the reader and create a choppy, uneven rhythm.

Similar in effect are the "stamps" which retard or stop active narration. Lyric contemplation of nature produces a striking rhythmic contrast with the frenetic movement of man. The novel's rhythm may be compared to a poet running through a field, describing his every progress. Every few paces he is overcome by a glorious sight and must stop to capture its detail. If a reader is wont to merely follow plot, this start-stop rhythm is confusing, but once accustomed to the technique he will reap the thrill and serenity of the novelistic movement. This oscillation slows rhythm. The reader should not hurry to find out "what happened"; he must content himself with the beauties proffered through deliberate retardation.

Concentric narration is a further means of rhythmic control.

Past mixes with present; one character's actions complement or explain those of another; the narrator repeatedly backtracks to further delineate a particular character. Concentric progression also retards the action. The reader cannot skip lightly over any detail since all are part of a central unity. If he misses a bit of information the final circle will remain incomplete and rhythm will appear broken. While Godoy's prose rhythm is uneven, it is always complete. Concentric narration imparts balanced rhythm to the prose.

PLOT. Godoy's plot structure—the temporal and spatial sequence upon which the narrative is constructed—is usually subservient to poetic description and philosophical analysis. Events, or incidents, are secondary to ideology and lyric expression. In short, Godoy is not as concerned with *what* occurs as he is with *why* and *how*. This emphasis gives rise to a loosely woven plot. Main characters are not strong, heroic protagonists; most are antagonists (outside forces fight against them) or agonists (they fight against themselves). With this type of central figure, plot is ancillary to character conflict and psychological struggle.

Angurrientos, and indeed the whole movement it represents, is based on man's struggle against society and social norms. Plot is relatively simple; most of the characters conform to their miserable life. The single nonconformist is buffeted by reality until at last he, too, conforms. But Godoy portrays him as a hero—he has fought the good fight. Other characters are also heroic in loyalty and integrity. The plot is frequently broken, vague, and repetitious, as a result of intercalation, active and contemplative narration, and concentric progression. A reader may lose the thread of plot and have to regress to pick it up.

The incidents of the second novel are likewise simple. A boy observes and communicates with a blind man. The plot is given a dualistic nature as the child also follows the action of a drunken neighbor. In the second part of the novel, the two incidents are united as Golondrino presides at the bedside of Serafín, the neighbor. After the death, the plot follows Golondrino, who ascends the mountain and beyond. The conflict is man against man himself, represented by both the boy and the blind man.

In *Sangre de murciélago* man is again seen struggling with himself. The situation is complicated by alcohol, which controls the lives of the characters. Incidents of the plot are clear and simple; two alcoholics become good friends, relate their past lives, seek a cure, and leave the institution. With such simple structure, it is evident that, especially in this novel, plot serves other purposes.

Godoy's short stories resemble his novels in the simplicity of plot. One of the clearest examples of internal conflict superseding plot is "El gato de la maestranza" where the only real action of the story is the shooting of the cat in the final scene. The remainder is reflection, doubting and soul-searching. Conflicts in these short stories are generally man against himself or against other men.

Since suspense is normally dependent upon plot, and since plot is weak, Godoy utilizes other techniques to achieve suspense. Intercalation (postponement), dramatism, and fluctuation between picture and drama create the poised expectancy of suspense.

Unity of plot achieved in the author's prose is effected through concentric narration rather than through sequential order. One person, one place, and usually one temporal unit occupy the center of the stage. Around these unities the rest of the plot revolves. While the incidents that surround the midpoint may at first appear disjointed, their unity and meaning are soon evident, as they enrich and impart new light to the center stage. Unless viewed in this perspective, plot will appear chaotic in Godoy. Many incidents involving new, unrelated characters circumscribe the principal events of the plot. Stories such as the death of Pistolas' husband, the forced baptism and death of Wanda's grandmother, and the kidnapping of Miss Betty Peal from *Angurrientos* could seem extraneous if the reader fails to appreciate their value in enriching the created world.

The technique of ending the story is well wrought in Godoy. Instead of the dramatic, all-inclusive ending, he chooses another direction. The first novel is the most conclusive of the three, but even here much more must follow after the final word. Edmundo has pronounced a terse, confused discourse. Like the short stories, the ending is ironical; but it is not decisive. Edmundo now begins a new life but with more problems than before.

The last two works also leave the plot incomplete. They share in common the transformation of man into myth at the time of death. There is finality in the death of the antagonists at the novels' end, but each is allowed to exist beyond this life. While the man is gone, his influence and philosophy will endure. These inconclusive endings cause the reader to ponder and meditate the incidents of the plot, the novelistic world is still advancing.

CONCLUSION. Structure and form in Godoy are fresh and original. His nuances have startled some critics, but they mark the most essential values of his prose. With narrative parallelisms, psychological parentheses, interspersed fantasies, successive juxtapositions, lyric "stamps," and many other controls, Godoy severs himself from traditional forms of Chilean prose. His new creation is still a novel, but it is one which reproduces a more uneven, chaotic, more realistic view of life than that which resulted from the ordered artificiality of previous novels. His expansion of novelistic limits is one of his major contributions to Chilean literature.

Sangre de murciélago is the most structurally disjointed of all the author's works. Its concentric narration revolves around present time, but generously interweaves events from the immediate and distant past. Thus, novelistic form reflects and becomes an acute amalgamation: "The novel was written in fragments, in notebooks, on book covers, on scraps of paper. With Godoy this is a habit, a technique. For this reason there is parallelism in his works, short scenes, long chapters, etc. He's difficult to follow but once accustomed, the reader cannot leave his shadow, such a Chilean but at the same time universal shadow. The shadow of the true artist."[30]

Loosed from the bonds of conventional narrative, Godoy writes freely, achieving flexibility and innovation in the novel. He incorporates short stories into long narrative to complement and add depth to the universe. Alternation between active and lyric narration slows the progression of the prose and creates an uneven, start-and-stop rhythm. "Stamps" lend poetic elegance to an otherwise sordid world. Godoy's formal control and structural innovations merit him a deserved place among Chile's literary elite.

VII   *Time*

"Time in literature always refers to elements of time as given in experience."[31] But time in literature is *not* time in experience. An author employs technical conventions which allow a month or a year to pass in one sentence. Even though a writer, of necessity, uses experiencable elements of time—an hour, a day, a clock, a setting sun—his esthetic transformation of these elements gives distinctive meaning to his particular work.

In Chilean Criollism time is marginal, and secondary to plot development. Rarely is time distorted for artistic purposes; a logical, orderly sequence prevails. It is primitive time, as shown in Latorre's *Zurzulita*; its passing is marked by the change of seasons. Time assumes primacy in Godoy's prose, reflecting new concern for man and the effect of time upon him. Problems of time have been concisely examined in the previous chapter on verbal complexes and, in this chapter, under concentric narration. However, many other conclusions result from careful investigation.

Compression is the first temporal principle of Godoy's prose output. Many events are crowded into a period of a day or a few hours. This is a departure from the former literary school, where months or years pass, according to the exigencies of plot logic. The action of the entire first part of *Angurrientos* transpires in three short time periods—a morning, siesta time, and an evening. There are no indications that these are periods of separate days; it is simply *a* day. In the experience of the poor, where today is no different from yesterday and tomorrow is identical with today, there is little necessity to portray a lapse of months or years. One day—any day—in the commoner's life can typify his misery and despair. As the second part of the novel commences, the narrator appraises his audience that eight long weeks have passed and Ovalle is now sick. But the reader still cannot effect a temporal location—eight weeks may have passed since the first part, or it may be an eight-week span two years later. He immediately perceives that, whatever period has elapsed, no significant change has been wrought by time. Characters, surroundings, and responses are identical to those of the first part. Again, all events occur in one day and in the early hours of the following morning. Temporal activity is compressed into less than forty-eight hours in the entire novel.

The dramatic series of events in the second novel takes place in a three-hour period on the Night of San Juan and early the next morning. An indefinite past is included to give background and to deepen meaning. Of the three novels, *Sangre de murciélago* covers the longest period but is still temporally compressed. The action occurs over a summer, a fall, and a winter; but only three days are viewed in depth. A conversation of a few hours' time constitutes the entire first part of the novel. In the second part, several days pass imperceptibly, with no distinction between one day and the next. The only differentiation is between weekdays and weekends. Weekends mean drink and sex; weekdays are dry and loveless. The final part occurs in a single day, following a twelve-week lapse. Again Godoy compresses his narrative movement into limited time periods.

The short stories similarly reduce the period of action to the briefest moment. In most of them, similar to *La cifra solitaria,* an indefinite past provides background for the active time of narration. This dual temporal structure broadens the base for the action. Both temporal segments are active narration; important events transpire in each, but the first half sets the stage for the second. The most lucid case in point is "El gato de la maestranza." The first half of the story (25-32) identifies a broad, multiple field of action. Verbs are plural: "They loved it [the cat] deeply"; no single person assumes primacy—the cat is the center of attention, and time is general. A temporal shift is effected in the second segment (32-35). One man, the narrator, becomes the center of attention. Time is definite in this main action of the story: "I believe I must now declare . . . I killed the cat." The first part takes place over an extended, nondescript period of time; the second is compressed time—a few minutes only.

Disjointed temporal structure—a conspicuous quality in all Godoy's prose—is a second characteristic of his portrayal of time. The mingling of past with present in the third novel, the indefinite past time of the short stories, are all elements which sever temporal unity. Events from other times are introduced into the limited, compressed period of action in each novel. By so doing, Godoy expands upon theme and provides essential background information but destroys chronological relationships. Such seeming disorder in previous generations would have been unpardonable, but Godoy views the novel as a living, evolving entity. Man lives in a series of moments that slide into each other. One's own past, the past of his associates, and the present they all create coalesce into a new present, the present of human time. The effect, however disjointed, has been described as similar to an artist's painting:

The artist need not proceed regularly from one corner of the canvas to the other; he is under no obligation to finish one section before beginning on another, but is at liberty to distribute the strokes of his brush wherever he thinks fit. The order and precedence of his work is determined by him and him alone, just as the order and precedence of the act of seeing the picture, the movements of the eye of the viewer follow no fixed rule. The effect of the whole picture is felt when the whole is seen, not in a fixed order of succession. . . .[32]

A novelist, like a painter then, is free to order his work. If the whole is effective, the techniques must also be effective. Godoy describes a world where order does not prevail; hence, his form imitates his material. The total image projected by his created universe is one of jumbled confusion; temporal dis-unity is just one component of that image. In a world where dream, semiwakefulness, and drunken illusion are as real as blankets, beds, and bottles, the use of temporal dislocation is most appropriate. Time shift, interior monologue, start-and-stop techniques, and delaying the outcome of an action all blend to project a disjointed temporal concept in Godoy.

Various symbols in the author's works reflect temporal elements. These were enumerated and detailed in this chapter. Ashes symbolize the passing of time. Both the sea and sky are symbols of eternity, or negation of time.

A fourth and final principle of time in Godoy is an alignment with myth. Man transcends mortality and the normal boundaries of time. While the action of the work may be compressed into a few hours or days, values and meaning are too far-reaching for these limited time units. Thus, Godoy captures not only actions of today or last week but timeless moments. The poor commoner is given atemporal qualities, especially in the first novel. A telluric, symbolic linking of man with earth also demonstrates mythical method in Godoy. The popular, hallowed *tonadas, cuecas,* and picaresque songs further extend the temporal limits of the work.

In *La cifra solitaria* the central figure is completely transformed into myth. As the dramatic action concludes, Golondrino ascends, merging with sea and sky. As symbols of eternity in Godoy, the sea and sky render Golondrino immortal. The Night of San Juan, steeped in myth, provides the setting; and the reader is assured that every June 24 Golondrino will reappear. As Ordóñez dies at the end of *Sangre de murciélago* "his intel-

ligence ... ascended into heaven." This conclusion, similar to
the second novel except that only the agonist's brain transcends
this world, is mythical. Intellect is metamorphosed into myth.
A strong link with myth is the symbolism of wine. A significant
connection with Greek and Latin mythology is established;
Bacchus, Dionysus, and other classical figures have meaning in
the lives of the novelistic characters. Through these methods,
Godoy lifts man from the present, unites him with the past, and
endows him with eternal life.

Time in Godoy's prose is charged with significance for man.
The poor commoner is not a phenomenon of today, of last year,
or of 1640; he is an elevated, eternal being. Time does not affect
him. Characters such as Augusto, Amaranto, Ovalle, the narrator of *Sangre de murciélago* undergo no change from start
to finish. Thus, man becomes a symbol of continuity in time.
Time does not lead to death but to broader participation in
eternity.

VIII   *Space*

Just as time is compressed into the shortest possible moment,
so are spatial relationships confined to small quarters and narrow streets. *Angurrientos* commences in the dirty streets of an
enclosing ravine. The opening scenes of the second novel are
limited to a blind alley. *Sangre de murciélago* begins on a
narrow mountain road. *El impedido* occurs in a single room.
The world is confining and closed. Man is unalterably caught
in his small, closed world. But as each of the works progresses,
the world opens slightly, and new vistas are perceived. Man,
however, is unable to transcend space as he does time. The
reader usually sees just one neighborhood or section. Within this
confined world, there are rapid shifts of scene, similar to the
brisk temporal dislocations already mentioned. There are fourteen separate spatial locations in the first novel, with frequent
change and return to each:

1. The poverty ravine, next to the cemetery (9)
2. Interior of Augusto's house (13)
3. Interior of Amaranto's house (35)
4. Outside, in a field (43)
5. The bar, "Quinta de Recreo las Delicias" (55)
6. Cockfighting ring and surroundings (61)

During the first part of the novel the scene shifts rapidly. Then three extended scenes, the *rancho*, Ovalle on his deathbed, and Wanda's bedroom compose more than half the novel. An analysis of spatial shifts confirms the principle of concentric narration—Godoy returns regularly to the point from which a previous chapter or section began. The entire novel is a circle, opening with a scene in the street, contiguous to the cemetery, and concluding with Edmundo in a similar street scene. No lateral progression has been effected, only vertical analysis, into the interiors of the houses and lives of the street's inhabitants. Space is intensified rather than amplified.

The other novels also carry out frequent spatial shifts. *La cifra solitaria* begins in a shack on a poor, blind alley. Throughout the work, spatial horizons are continually expanded. Action moves from the shanty to an adjoining house and a view from a hilltop, then to neighboring streets, a bar on the other side of the river, to the woods, and finally to the mountains and sea. There is an ascending spatial progression; the world is expanded as the boy narrator grows and learns. The concluding scene encompasses the entire universe.

On a spatial plane, *Sangre de murciélago* is the most complex novel. Similar to its temporal fluctuation from present to past to present, spatial organization is an unremitting descent-ascent-descent pattern. "We *descended* the hill, laughing" (15), of the first chapter is countered with "we *climbed* the hill to get our robes, slippers, and towels" my italics (67) in the second. The shift from the institution to the town or bar, and then back to the establishment, creates a constant spatial oscillation. The novel concludes with a *descent,* man crushed by an accelerating train, in the city. The setting for the novel, however, is the entire country of Chile. There are approximately forty-five different scenes.

In the novels action moves principally through interior scenes;

the short stories alternate equally between indoors and outdoors:
there are indoor and outdoor scenes in each story. Movement
is generally from the broad arena of nature to the confinements
of indoors. Nature and wildlife in "El ramal" are the most vital
influences on the narrator's life. Outdoors, man is free to choose
and develop his soul. Unfortunately, most of the author's
characters spend too little time outdoors.

Godoy's scenes are most often confined to a house, a small
chamber, or a section of a room. In these enclosed arenas the
novel is intensified, and drama is heightened. Limited, cramped
space emphasizes conflict and tension. Thus, space functions as
an intensifier of action and plot. Limited space, with freedom
in time, creates a deeply dramatic novel.[33]

IX   *Folklore*

Despite complex metaphors, classical symbolism, ruptured
narrative structure, and occasional philosophizing, Godoy's appeal is not solely to learned readers. The inclusion of popular,
folkloric elements in each novel brings his literature to the masses.
The author views the common man as a complex union of cold
reality and poetic fantasy. To depict the infinite world of fantasy,
Godoy assimilates popular legends and songs.

The intercalated story of "The Ash-colored Cock" repeats the
legendary motif of man's miraculous transformation into animal.
In the tale, foreigners are winning at the cockfights, and Chile
is being humiliated. During the noon break a "dark olivaceous
giant-man" appears and offers a bizarre solution: he will turn
himself into a huge cock. He secretly effects the change, tri-
umphs over all the gringos, and promptly returns to his human
form. The motif is current throughout Chilean and world folklore. Glorification of the common man as a national hero adds
typical Chilean flavor.

A second popular story is the "Facico/Facica" affair. A mis-
chievous young Negro feigns the voice of revelation and tells
Facica she must sleep with him or "if not, the world will end,
devils and demons will appear." The girl falls for, and enjoys,
the deception. The fable originates in oral tradition. One of
Chile's leading folklore authorities believes that Juan Godoy
acquired the tale from his mother's treasury of stories.[34]

Eudoxia's fanciful story of Romoán is based upon the folkloric motif of the miraculous birth. The Virgin Mary blesses an

elderly, childless couple with a son. The baby weighs forty-five pounds at birth and becomes the scourge of the town as he grows beyond proportion. Forced to leave his home, he learns compassion and love among the forest animals, and a happy ending is conjectured. The story is totally removed from the events of the novel. Its purpose is the delineation of a single character, whom Godoy believes typical of the masses. Since the events of the story are Godoy's invention, they cannot be considered as folklore, but the theme is definitely a folkloric motif.

Golondrino himself is representative of a popular element. He carries with him the wisdom of the entire world. He possesses magical powers and is the only person who know the "twelve magic words." Upon the death of Serafín, Golondrino is called to ward off the devil, who attempts to claim the dead man's soul. Satan, as the interlocutor, asks for certain responses. Golondrino must repeat, without error, the twelve signs and their meaning. Twelve questions and responses are given, each previous answer being repeated with the succeeding ones. Golondrino is successful, and Serafín's soul is saved. Godoy effects a minor change in the traditional format of the "magic words." The devil's presence is felt, but he does not actually appear, so the men at the wake voice his questions. This motif is common throughout most of the world. " 'Magic words' are used as an entreaty and according to legend are infallible. They are recited only in times of great need."[35] Unlike the story which Eudoxia tells, the folklore of the "twelve words" is woven into the narrative thread of the novel. They are vital to an understanding of the novel and represent the most dramatic moment of the work.

Two stories of popular appeal enhance *Sangre de murciélago*. The bat-blood cure is Godoy's own creation, but once again, it is built upon a folkloric motif. A paterfamilias forsakes home and wife as a result of drink. In misery, he seeks a cure and, after a two-day fast, is graciously served a cup of bat's blood. He is not only cured but is transformed into an adolescent. The supernatural restoration of youth is the motif which popularizes the story. As Godoy's invention it exemplifies the coalescence of folklore and artistic creation as well as the mythological relationship with Bacchus.

The second story, "The Buzzard," is a popular ballad, told in the deformed speech of country peasant. The simple tale is Godoy's fabrication; a buzzardlike hired hand spoils the dignity of his master's party by putting nails in the biscuits. The narrator of the brief account is one of the inmates of the institution. He represents the common worker, for he associates with intellectuals and artists. His story is merely characterization of his own personality rather than advancement of the narrative.

Many other evidences of folklore and popular expression abound in Godoy's prose. A fighting cock dies from the evil eye (*Angurrientos,* 92). The morbid irony of "All the Lice Drowned" is one of popular origin. The distorted speech of the commoner is frequently reproduced. Popular sayings are common. The "little mother" story from *Sangre de murciélago* embraces several popular features. The whole concept of personal involvement in cockfighting reflects the mien of low society. Every work exudes the language or experience of the masses.

Despite the above appraisals, Godoy is not a folklorist. His literature is more than a medium for the preservation of traditional customs. The popular stories, songs, and expressions advance a narrative already in progress. In most instances, they are thoroughly integrated and become an essential part of the story. Folklore, or, as Godoy prefers, popular expression, is not extraneous, but richly enhances the quality of his prose. In fact, the nature of his works prescribes the inclusion of such folkloric elements. A literature so involved with the life of the *roto* could only be hollow without the flavor of the myth and folklore so much a part of Chilean culture.

X *Conclusion*

The study of style and technique is absolutely necessary for even a beginning comprehension of Juan Godoy, due to the numerous complexities involved. These two aspects of his prose have shown that Godoy creates a literary world that is *not* an authentic reflection of the real world. He perceives reality with his poetic sensitivity and produces a new sphere, altered by lyric subjectivity. To what he perceives with his senses he adds dimensions of comparison through metaphor, intensification through imagery, and poetry through alliteration, rhythm, and so on. "He blurs clarity, obscures precision, and applies a pinch of dream to reality. Run-down slums, therefore, take on poetic qualities."[36]

While Godoy's themes classify him as a Neo-Realist, his style does not meet the normal standards of Realism. When equated with other Latin American literary movements, his style approaches that of the Expressionists; his themes draw near to literary Realism. The combination is an intriguing blend of psychological penetration and social involvement, bringing enjoyment to the reader. Enrique Anderson Imbert eulogizes this dualism for the universal effects it achieves: "Juan Godoy is also concerned with the common man. . . . In Godoy, more than Nicomedes Guzmán, one recognizes a style common to many contemporary Spanish-American novelists: naturalistic and socialistic themes painted with poetic rhythm, seen through the eyes of frequent metaphor, glimpsed in numerous surrealistic dreams, moved with the nonconventional techniques similar to Aldous Huxley or James Joyce."[37]

Godoy passes over no opportunity to bring poetry to his prose. The foregoing examination of style and technique easily justifies the tag "poetic prose" affixed to Godoy's works. Yet no one device, metaphor for example, poeticizes his writing; rather, the whole range of verbal complexities and innovative, nonrealistic techniques combine to heighten expression. All elements function together. Characterization, where possible, is effected through metaphor and artistic association. Poetic characters, those extracted from realms of fantasy or folklore, appear in every work. The intercalcation of verse and short stories strengthens the sensation of poetry in prose. The contemplative "stamps" create a synesthetic effect, bringing elements from the plastic arts to prose. Dreams relieve the oppression of the real world and draw forth the subconscious. Folkloric aspects lend poetic stature. A rhythm more akin to poetry than prose strengthens the lyric quality of the works.

Godoy is occasionally accused of being too poetic; his prose is: "More lyric than dramatic. . . . Language for language's sake cripples the novel. . . . It produces feelings rather than solutions."[38] Some feel the poetic nature of the prose impedes novelistic progression. Such may be the case, but, as has been shown, Godoy chooses to penetrate deeply rather than pass superficially over creation to final judgment. The whole action of *La cifra solitaria* takes place in a few hours; narrative action is minimal while poetic intensification assumes primacy. This is not a defect; it is simply a type of prose which differs from Naturalistic works. Teitelboim's accusation quoted above is further weakened by understanding that verbal complexes harmonize and complement meaning. Hence, style is not an ornamentation but an integral part of narration. Godoy's work is true prose with the beauty of verse. It is high prose, poetic prose, in the style of Joyce and Faulkner; as such it is lasting literature; time enhances its value.

CHAPTER 4

Man–An Agonized Existence

FROM the spongy obesity of worthless politicians, or the swollen gangrenous leg stump of El Cojín, to the deified Golondrino ascending heavenward, man is the center of Godoy's novelistic universe. *Man is a struggling, agonized being, striving to raise himself from misery to decency and nobility.* This one vital theme imparts unity to the author's entire prose output.

The topics of the previous chapters are of minor importance if unrelated to theme. If there is no unifying generalization about life, no controlling idea or insight implied in the story, style is merely embellishment and technique is hollow. But in Godoy, style and technique support and complement the portrayed view of life, and understanding of theme clarifies seeming incongruities of certain verbal complexes and narrative techniques.

One of the prime objectives of the generation of 1938 was to "portray the men of this country, as part of Latin America and part of humanity." The novelist felt the pressing "necessity to unite with the masses, the workers, to uncover absolute being and concrete society."[1] Godoy sought a common, unifying aspect in humanity—an expression of the soul of universal man. He was not satisfied merely to depict a Chilean type, with no extranational reverberations. The country *huaso,* overdrawn and stereotyped, somewhat like the North American cowboy, was too regionally limited to express universality. The hardened *roto,* on the other hand, was not static or legendary, but a vital, oppressed human being (more akin to the courageous, struggling pioneer than to the cowboy, if a comparison can be made). His plight epitomized humanity's plight; his life offered untapped inspiration for artistic creation.

Godoy deals little with physical aspects of man's reality. The external contests of the continent, the wars of independence, are history; twentieth-century heroic man has psychological and moral battles to win, problems of identity and spiritual separa-

121

tion to conquer. A discerning critic of Latin American prose, effecting comparison with world literature, has observed that: "The basis for European and even North American narrative is, in reality, man in himself, with his internal complexities and moral problems.... It is, therefore, essentially a psychological literature with universal meanings. Spanish-American literature, on the other hand, is predominantly environmental, landscape and sociological."[2]

Godoy sagaciously avoids overemphasis of landscape, concentrating primarily on inner feelings, and secondarily on man's relationship to his often oppressive environment. Just as physical man is not foremost in Godoy, physical surroundings are secondary to spiritual conflict. Though man is seen working and interacting with the land, it is not Godoy's major emphasis.

Enrique Anderson Imbert has indiscriminately grouped Francisco Coloane, Nicomedes Guzmán, Fernando Alegría, and Reinaldo Lomboy in the category of social novelists. His criteria would classify Godoy in the same order. "In Chile, the line of writers with social aims was not interrupted since here the connection between man and his environment is more important than man himself."[3] But Godoy's aims are not purely social. More important than society in general is the individual human within the populace. While society must be included in a portrayal of man's totality, Godoy's theme is the individual, not society as a whole. It is supposed that, as the individual advances, society will similarly progress upward, but the latter consideration is secondary.

Some literary critics have observed the recent trend of Chilean prose to focus on universal, man-centered themes, rather than on regional, stereotyped expression. "Chile, one of the South American countries most obstinate about shaking off the old fetters of Criollism, is also beginning to show signs of going along with this important literary transition ... new novelists are trying to discover what is in the minds of those tenement dwellers."[4] Godoy blazes the rough trail from previous literature to an era of deeper penetration into man's soul. He selects the huddled, boisterous ambience of poverty pockets. In such unhappy surroundings, man—inhibited, violent, and passionate— struggles for meaning and purpose. The new prose is artistic, yet it cultivates the ugly, the horrible, and the disorderly. Thus, by means of an artistic, elevated style, Godoy envisions man plagued by misery and abject lowliness. Life is a perpetual contest with tribulation and sorrow.

I *The Anguish of Life*

In Godoy, man—be he beggar, child, politician, or professor—experiences affliction and anguish. But Godoy's anguish must not be confused with Existential anguish, as formulated by Kierkegaard. For the Danish philosopher, anguish is the expression of spiritual vertigo when faced with various alternatives pointing to salvation and eternal happiness. Implied is that choices exist in life and that free will leads to anguish. Man perceives his existence as "an unjustified moment. . . . His being is questionable in relationship to the divine absolute."[5] Godoy's use of the term *angustia* more closely parallels that of Unamuno. The word *congoja,* which includes anxiety, grief, and affliction as well as anguish, more fully represents Godoy's concepts. In contrast to Kierkegaard, and like Unamuno, anguish in Godoy "has nothing to do with the revelation of an unjustified being, rather, with the experience of a being treading thin ice."[6] Godoy's characters are spared the ethical-religious conflicts found in Kierkegaard; the concept of sin is absent from his works. Similar in their rejection of any belief in God and sin are contemporary Existentialists, who also expound concepts of man's nothingness and unjustified existence. In this light, the anguish in Godoy's creations is not existential. His men are significant, struggling beings, searching for meaning in existence. Although beset by afflictions, they are capable of advancement, of warmth, of love. Their existence is justified through their agonized fight for amelioration.

Man's anguish springs from multiple sources. First is the oppressing fear and trepidation of life. Neighbors incite fear; the humanized weather and landscape create terror in man; the unknown world disquiets the fearful heart; and finally, within himself, man finds inhibition, hatred, revenge, and insecurity, which further heighten fear. Against a backdrop of unremitting rain, the boy Loncho is anguished: "It rains torrentially. The rain saddens me as if it were filling my blood, my nerves, my life, with moss. Fear feeds our soul: fear brings the night, fear of murdered bodies in the alleys, fear of shadows, fear of the dead, of the spirits of the dead, of bandits, of unbearable winters. Door chains position our fear.... And the candle cries fear and its little light is filled with fear"(*La cifra solitaria,* 15, 16). Terror and fear, brought on by the rain, grow in the boy's soul until there is room for little else. Constant repetition of the word "fear" heightens his terror; like the incessant rain, it continually falls on the boy. And like the rain, it penetrates to the soul. The entire novel is structured around scenes of horror and fear. Drunken Serafín stabbing his submissive wife, the dark death wake with its frightful noises and satanic aura, and Golondrino in the rain and lightning are all scenes of extreme fear, especially for an unlearned boy. Dread, fright, terror and fear, often-repeated terms in Godoy, express the psychological state of many characters.

In *Sangre de murciélago* fear intensifies the anguish of numerous characters. Ordóñez relates from "memory" the appearance of Halley's comet, an event which occurred shortly *before* his birth. He "recalls" the fright of all concerned: "People massed in the streets, kneeling... asking God for mercy." His mother shrugs the incident off, saying "You couldn't see our fear." But Ordóñez interprets, "Perhaps, three months old, in the belly of my mother, I too cried out for mercy, before falling into the fear of this world" (127-28). For the incurable alcoholic, earthly existence is fraught with dreadful fears. His dreams, his flight from reality, his self-absorption all reveal the frightful anxiety of his world.

Edmundo, tormented by his mediocrity, in semiwakefulness, questions his own existence. As he awakens, "an absurd fear overcame his whole being, as if he were sailing through unknown seas.... He hoped someone would call him by name" (*Angurrientos,* 95). To allay his fears and confirm his existence he must hear his name spoken aloud. His apprehensions lead to irresolution and inaction; life is clouded with anguished doubt. "At times an uncontrollable fear blocked all action, fearing that any action would be his last" (98).

Man's most oppressive fears, however, are not engendered by exterior violence, nature's turbulence, or superstition. Fear of being, or of becoming, lodged deep in the soul, is man's most profound anguish. Outside forces play little role in this fear; man creates it within himself. The narrator of *La cifra solitaria* postulates: "Man finds being in death.... And there is deep fear of becoming, not of nothingness" (57). Neither does the anticipation of death and the nothingness beyond generate real fright. Man's penetrating fears are of merely being, living, existing; his perversity, anger, irresponsibility, lack of reason and self-control restrain him from ever actually being. Fears suppress his existence. As Ovalle writhes on his deathbed, he analyzes his life: "I feared life.... I did not act. Because I did not want to be" (*Angurrientos*, 219). The narrator interrupts the anguished thought to philosophize: "There are, as I see it, three ways to become: (1) struggling forward, (2) remaining firm in a denial of action, and (3) simply killing oneself" (219). But all three choices incite fear in Ovalle, who resigns his life to fate and soon dies.

Edmundo, Wanda, Loncho, Nacha, Ordóñez, and the narrator of *El impedido* are all oppressed by powerful inner fears. Only Wanda overcomes fear, decapitates a fighting cock, and becomes something. "She had killed a myth.... She didn't understand her action but felt freed to face life" (*Angurrientos*, 240). Thus, in Godoy, being is achieved by routing the inner fears which thwart action.

A second source of anguish is solitude and loneliness, which eventually leads to alienation. Man is alone in the world, fearfully trapped within himself. He is a *lonely cipher*. Symbolic of all mankind, Golondrino gropes blindly, alone in perpetual darkness. He speaks, but no one understands; blindness separates him from the physical world; his own daughter fails to recognize her father. His mute dog as his only companion, Golondrino gradually leaves his cold ambience and eventually severs himself from the earth.

Golondrino's anguished loneliness is not peculiar. All of Godoy's men are alone. If married, they do not communicate with their spouses. The life of one character means little or nothing to his neighbor. Even in *Sangre de murciélago* Ordóñez and his talking companion, who seem to establish a firm friendship, do not communicate; each remains locked in his own tight world. There is no interplay, mutual help, or compassion. The narrator accepts Ordóñez' death without emotion, an event as common as crossing the street. The two are components of different worlds. This final novel abounds with characters who live together but remain alone, isolated from involvement. Man, even in a crowd, is tragically alone. Jobet feels that man in this novel has given up his struggle for betterment and withdrawn from social existence.[7]

Humberto, Horacio, and Edmundo of the first novel "were orphans in their own country, wandering alone, owning nothing" (127). "Man dies alone, frightfully alone, in fearful loneliness. ... But how joyous death would be side by side with a brother, our brother, in heroic action" (148). But there is no heroic brother to befriend. A favorite word in the first novel is *huacho*, which Godoy defines as "an orphan, without a known father, alone," symbolizing spiritual alienation as well as parental neglect. Although many social relationships are established in Godoy's prose, man is still a solitary being. Wanda has parents and a brother; Edmundo has friends and a sweetheart; Ordóñez has a wife, lover, and admirers; yet each experiences deep personal alienation. Godoy's characters never escape the anguish of their self-imposed solitude.

The author's short stories offer the most poignant illustrations of anguished loneliness. The professor has aged and retired. His students still remember him but have outgrown his influence. In Godoy's prose he is a hero, one of the very few who "swallow personal pride and struggle for the success of others" (52). His active, selfless participation in life and his ability to get outside himself bring nobility to his soul. But his compassion leads to disaster. He is attacked by a band of young thieves, robbed, knocked down, and loses his glasses. At this moment, alone, beaten by boys who should have been his pupils, and symbolically blind, his soul is pained: "He was broken, fleeced, lost in a stupor. Completely alone on the bridge ... with the despair of a teacher who never had such students in his hands" ("El profesor," 59-60).

Inner torment provides the foundation for Godoy's most compassionate short story, "The Whip." An untamed youth has little dealing with people and seeks constant refuge in nature. His relationships with human playmates bring only sorrowful deception and anguish. At a party, he permits another to see his wild canary: "He took the cage and all the other children formed a circle around him, leaving me alone. In life I have always been excluded from inner circles, alone ..." (122).

Various critics have linked Godoy's prose to French literary school of Unanimism and listed him as a disciple of Jules Romains.[8] This observation stems principally from *Angurrientos,* where the common interest in cockfighting supposedly unites the owners in brotherhood. According to Unanimism, group characteristics are more vital in shaping conduct than are the attitudes and beliefs of the individual. If this were completely true in Godoy, man would not suffer the anguish of loneliness and alienation; the group to which he belongs would provide companionship, understanding, and fraternity. Although cockfighting does provide a common bond, each person is a loner, more absorbed in himself than in the group. Edmundo drinks alone. Ovalle dies alone. Augusto simply disappears on a dreary street. The death of Amaranto's rooster leaves him to his solitude. The characters of *Sangre de murciélago* have only one common attribute—each is an incurable alcoholic. Their unity is merely situational; when they leave the institution they feel no collective spirit. Unanimism is present, but only vaguely in Godoy; it cannot override man's alienation and lonely withdrawal into self.

Loneliness (*soledad*), like fear, is an internal sensation. Godoy's concern is the suffering of inner man, not "man-male" or "man-hero" of earlier literature in Chile. *Soledad* has long been a theme in Spanish poetry; its usage in Godoy is one further link in his chain of poetic prose. Man is not a gregarious, commingling entity; anguish thrives in his lonely soul.

A third component of anguish in Godoy is failure. Man's struggle for decency most frequently ends in frustration. Success— overcoming anguish and improving one's lot—*is* possible, as evidenced by Wanda and Golondrino. But endeavor commonly leads to impasse. Edmundo's entire search is a struggle against mediocrity, an attempt to become something greater than friends and surroundings dictate. His tragic conformity at the novel's end has already been detailed. Ovalle escapes anguish only when he possseses a winning cock (80), but his roosters most frequently lose, and he is blighted by agony and distress. Golondrino also fails to light any life but his own. Most penetrating are the sorrowful failures of the alcoholics in the third novel. The narrator candidly admits that through cunning he has avoided the painful treatments. He simply enjoys a "vacation" at the institution, escaping the real purpose of his commitment. He returns, more depraved than before, to the anguish of alcohol. In short, he has decided to fail. Even those who direct the Institute of Mental Reeducation are failures. The psychiatrist

128 JUAN GODOY

confesses: "The truth is, I have never been able to cure anyone" (34).

The element of anguish is inherent in Angurrientist philosophy. Moderation is impossible; the hungry one must empty his platter at one sitting. Little provision is made for the morrow. Life is redundant with excesses. Anxiety is the logical consequence. Wine in abundance causes drunkenness. Gluttony today provides nothing for tomorrow. Betting and losing all on the cockfights leaves no money for new breeding and betting. Herminia's death is attributed to overindulgence. Serafín's drunken orgies hasten his death. Alcoholics of the last novel suffer from lack of control and insatiable desires. Man drinks himself into bankruptcy.

Godoy's symbolism focuses on man, revealing his anguished existence. The symbol, an outward sign, always refers to an interior anxiety or emotion in Godoy. Symbols are revelations of man's inner life. By using symbols in this manner, Godoy succinctly captures a character's soul. The ox symbolizes man's pain and suffering, a spiritual rather than a physical anguish engendered by fate and alienation. Disunion and separation from positive, primitive forces are inherent in the symbol of the root. Man has lost the powers previously extant in the world and is now rootless. The sky is symbolic of man's quest for the infinite, his anguished desire to transcend mortality. Ashes mark the passing of time and the mental torment of life's instability. Similar in scope is man's irrepressible yearning for the timeless expanses of the sea. He is separated from his succor and must live tormented, in time. Incomprehension of self is symbolized by the mirror; man perceives only a minute segment of his being. Light symbolizes goodness and truth, originating within man. When light is absent, as it usually is in Godoy, the agony of spiritual blindness results. Although wine may produce and also symbolize man's irrational behavior, causing him pain and suffering, it is nevertheless a positive symbol. It links man to the past and to the earth which engenders telluric powers. Wine also represents one means of escape from man's distress, if used in moderation.

Through dream, the anguish of man's subconscious is shared with the reader. In this manner the narrator exposes an otherwise hidden segment of human existence. Dreams in Godoy portray torment and affliction. The dream of the youth in "The

Whip" is one of fear and agony. The climax finds the boy "hanging over a cliff, holding onto the bloody foot of Christ" (126). Faith in God, a rare quality in Godoy, delivers him from torment. Other characters, especially those in *Sangre de murciélago*, are less fortunate. Despite its humor, the dream of the missing liver unveils neurotic fear. The disintegrating body and the persecution by the dead soldier likewise betray internal fears not banished at daybreak. The transformation of the grapevine, first into an enticing sensual woman and then into a withered, repulsive man, communicates the deception of the world. Man, in distress, undergoes profound anxiety as he realizes the instability of his environs. Mutilation and destruction characterize the dream of the otter which masticates the horse and that of the headless, rubber beings. In both instances, a vital part of the body is dismembered: testicles in the first; the head in the second. This ruthless mutilation discloses a fear of losing essential body parts, especially those of virility. The concluding dream reveals a trait which plagues most of Godoy's anguished characters— indecision. While protecting a young maiden, the dreamer is caught between opposing troops. He must choose a loyalty and enter into battle. Instead, "I was undecided while others died in the clash of arms" (231). Agony intensifies as man eludes decision, refusing to wholeheartedly enter the battle of life. In the dream neither side is victorious; both merely enjoy life and action. He who tarries in indecision lets life pass him by.

The tragedy occurs as the dreamer awakens and finds that his afflictions still plague him. Man's anguish in dream is merely a reflection of the real world. Fear, alienation, failure, overindulgence, and indecision are the components of this anguish. But man is not merely a cluster of negativity; Godoy envisions change and improvement. "That is to say, his works do not produce the persistent negative monotony that devitalizes so many other current novels."[9]

Man strives for love, success, and a fullness of life, but these positive qualities are normally trodden under by his own fears. Only in *El impedido* is man fully able to conquer fear and anxiety. The struggle for betterment, be it successful or not, liberates Godoy's prose from the negativism of other contemporary writers, particularly the Existentialists. Godoy's works express certain qualities of Existentialism: alienation, indecision at a host of choices. But the negativism, ennui, nausea, and absurdity of Existentialism are not present in his prose. Although fear and failure suppress and anguish man, there are always positive qualities to ennoble and encourage change. Life is perpetual striving rather than passive resignation to existence.

II *Escaping Anguish*

Despite inhibitions and negative qualities within, man endeavors to free himself from anguish. The methods he employs are usually exterior, originating from without, and hence, destined to failure. The first alternative for escape is sex. Man seeks woman not so much for love as for sex. Instead of relief, sex creates more anguish, debasing man instead of edifying him. Augusto recalls his Luz Dina: "Her slender thighs ... led him along the path to hot moss, to the irrevocable, to the red spider of her sex, to the anguish of self" (*Angurrientos*, 28). Both the agonists of *Sangre de murciélago* leave the unselfish love of their wives and seek mistresses. In both instances relief from anguish is temporary, and sex only adds to the mental torture. One refers to his regular visits to Sheva as "our daily death" and realizes that only as she sleeps may he love her without torment. Sex "was our habitual way of life, of suffering, of death" (98). The immediate fleeting joy is overshadowed by the deeply rooted anguish of life. Ovalle best exemplifies the incongruity and anguish resulting from sex. He experiences, almost simultaneously, love and hatred for his wife. Sex does not fulfill, and thus, cannot extricate mental distress; it leads to hatred.

The failure of sex to alleviate man's anguish arises from a fundamental concept in Godoy's philosophy. In sex, man seeks an external resolution to his agony. Godoy's prose demonstrates the need for man to interiorize, to search within self for solution and betterment. Sex alone will always lead to frustration, since it is an exterior, temporary postponement of anguish. Don Antón, the hero of "The Professor," possesses most of the positive qualities Godoy would inculcate in man. On a sensuous, warm night, with its colored lights and inviting perfumes, Antón is propositioned: "'Let me make you happy,' spoke the lacerated night, or Marimba, flowing all over him ..." (41). His response communicates the essentials of Godoy's theme: "No, you could not make me happy.... How could you make me happy when you are not?" (42). Don Antón's refusal and kind reprimand is a challenge to first search one's own soul. The acceptance of Marimba's invitation would lead only to sexual anguish.

A second possibility for escape is wine. Man drinks to escape the anguish of the present. As previously discussed, wine serves as a symbol, linking man with the past (myth) and with the land (tellurism). In moderation it possesses salutory powers, inciting joy, overriding restrictive inhibitions, evoking traditional songs and dances, and inspiring awarenes of self. Wine is gratifying and ennobling; it calls forth the inner man, and Godoy endows it with positive qualities.

But in excess, wine destroys these reputable characteristics and turns on man. The obstacle in the line of all Godoy's men is their inability to stop drinking at the proper moment. Drink controls them, and they lose mastership. Thus drink, like sex, does not resolve human anguish, but usually intensifies it. Drunkenness subverts reason and destroys the will to improve. "Edmundo had tried to get the drunks to give up their stupid lives as beasts of burden, planting rebellion in them, showing them their rights, dragging them into battle (*Angurrientos,* 47). But desire to drink has overcome desire to improve. No change is possible.

Edmundo avidly seeks change and self-knowledge, but he too falls into drink and ultimately tumbles headlong into nothingness. Horacio, Humberto, El Cojín, and others are wasted in drink. Loncho views drunken Serafín "filled with anguish."

The alcoholics in Godoy's third novel spend hours and weeks philosophizing on the injurious effects of wine, but they still indulge. Their friendships cause temporary suppression, but their basic nature, especially when alone, is anguish. "We surrounded ourselves with intimate friends . . . and we forgot our anguish" (81). But the relief is only fleeting; tomorrow man will be alone. As problems mount, the irresolutes seek refuge in wine. It is the easiest choice but always leads to deeper estrangement and anxiety. Ordóñez admits: "The emotional battle raging in my soul found relief in the wine of the first bar" (226).

The positive quality of wine—its ability to link man with earth and myth—is subverted by man's own lack of control. Once again, the problem lies within man, not without. In Godoy wine is good, but man corrupts its virtue. Godoy's use of a Latin phrase expresses both the joys and anguish of wine: *"Vinus opus Dei, ebrietas opus daemonis."*

If sex and wine are the only solutions to anguish, both of these being deceptive and granting no deliverance, then Godoy's men are tragic. Yoked in a strangling harness, they are consigned to a tragic existence over which they have no sovereignty. Many critics have pointed to the tragic nature of man in Godoy: "We are tragic beings and Godoy never passes a chance to remind us of the tragedy housed in our souls.... In this young Chilean we find the essence of our people who only have the brutal grasp of sex and alcohol to provide hope from tragic orphanhood."[10] In support of the tragic life of man is Godoy's frequent use of the word *destino*. But in the author's works the term usually denotes "fate," "destination," or "logical outcome." It does not imply an impersonal, tragic sense of destiny which capriciously controls man's life.[11] Man *is* capable of change; the power to change is within him. If he fails to avoid danger and encounters pain, it is most frequently the result of his own action. Serafín appears to be most directly in the hands of destiny. But even he is free; his death is a logical consequence of wine and anger. He chooses to drink, to cross the bridge, to enter the bar, and to incite his assassin. The alcoholics of *Sangre de murciélago* suffer from their own sins, not from whims of destiny.

Man in Godoy is not tragic; neither is he predestined. There is no tragedy, since fate is not operative. Man's life is his own choosing. Godoy allows various outlets from anguish. Love, as opposed to mere sex, is capable of replacing anxiety with joy. But unselfish, sincere love is rare in his works. Children, more than adults, show a capacity for loving and being loved. The youth in "The Whip" is Godoy's most graphic example of love conquering anguish. After the loss of his wild canary, the child suffers a dream of horrible anguish. Upon awaking, his grief mounts, driving him to leave home. He knows that if he is caught he will receive the whip. The following day an older brother finds him sleeping in a cave. Tension builds as the boy imagines his punishment, and upon entering the house he notices that the whip is lying on the table. In sobs he approaches his stern father, who "Gently took my head. He took me into his heart, ... and embracing me, chastised my face with the lash of his own tears" (129).

A second solution to the anxieties of life is self-realization. Light, truth, and goodness come from man's soul. Externals— sex, wine—are of little value. Only through interiorization— knowledge of self and illumination of his own soul—is man able to subdue anguish. This concept is basic in Godoy's philosophy of man. The only external capable of imparting joy is a communion with nature, and even this is dependent on man's receptiveness, since nature is unchanging in Godoy. Thus, power and truth are within man; life is complete and free from anxiety only when he discovers his own strength.

The enigmatic Edmundo, fighting against mediocrity, yearns to be a hero. And heroism, he realizes, begins within self. He nurtures the "powerful bud" but is defeated by alcohol and withers in mediocrity. His struggle, however, is valiant; he nearly overcomes anguish but allows external forces to subvert and destroy inner truth, perishing in conformity.

Wanda, on the contrary, finds interior strength, frees herself from the fetters of her surroundings by killing the cock, and uncovers spiritual beauty: "She now found a strong budding of light in an obscure corner of her own soul. And her soul was touched by life's kiss, a tender sprout of light in the immense soul of the world" (237).

In the above examples light is equated with truth and understanding of one's own soul and originates within self. The world is dark, and man is blind. Only through each man's realization of self will light spread through the world. Godoy's prose "exudes the symbolism of man living in eternal darkness yet finding the paradise of his own interior light."[12] Golondrino, walking in blindness, symbolizes all humanity. But unlike most other mortals, he finally discovers light and realizes his own potentialities. A drop of light filters through his "dead eyes," and "in his mind there was light . . . " (*La cifra solitaria*, 98). Throughout all of Godoy's prose there is constant orientation toward inner light. Man, not society or God, is to blame if the soul remains in darkness. Inner man is full of grace and beauty.

Anguish is a personal, interior sensation. Remedies external to man, such as exemplified by sex and wine, cannot subdue it. Only through knowledge of self and nurturing of inner light can man hope to cast out anguish and free himself from fears, inhibition, indecision, mediocrity, and loneliness.

III   *Man and Nature*

Godoy's ambitions for his prose demand creation and exposition of the soul of a universal man. The superficial incursions of Criollism were too narrow and regionalistic. The country *huaso*, Godoy feels, is limited, a caricature who extracts his wealth solely from the land. Conversely, the hardened commoner is capable of heroism, for he finds strength within himself. The image of this real type provides the prototypal man of Godoy's prose. Man in literature, rather than being a regionalistic stereotyped entity, should be a dynamic force, bound to the other men of his continent and of the world. The hardened commoner, Godoy believes, is the expression of universal man. Godoy deems it necessary to develop the relationship between man and the universe rather than man in a given region. Two specific Godoyan techniques reconcile his literary creations with American and universal values. First is his development of man's complex relationship with nature; the second, to be discussed in the following section, is his wide use of mythical method.

The entire American continent, Godoy feels, coalesces in a "single telluric entity."[13] Or, "America must now discover her own soul, her lost telluric-human unity" (*Angurrientos*, 132). By establishing an affinity between humanity and nature, Godoy extends man's horizons from his confined, natal valley to the illimitable reaches of the continent. The Chilean, his soul in communication with the land, parallels the experiences and develops similar traits to the Mexican; they are attuned to the same whisperings. Thus, the anguish and suffering of one man is the affliction of man everywhere. Man is more than an insignificant, limited being; he is endowed with ennobling, universal powers.

That man may more fully effect a union with the earth, Godoy humanizes the soil, the mountains, and the sea. When man is isolated and rejected by fellow man, he finds solace in the land, for it is alive and hospitable:

Long, hard, stout drops of rain. The brown body of earth breathed forth a smell of sex. (*Angurrientos*, 59)

And on the fig trees, the drop of honey hanging from the flesh of the ripe figs, as the swelling of a woman's sex. Wise with intuition the avid, burning, intoxicated earth bathes with her sun the semen of the fig. (*Angurrientos*, 61)

With the first rains, the earth emitted an acrid, enticing harmonious fragrance . . . . (*La cifra solitaria,* 39)

fields bursting with fruit trees and vineyards, their heads bowed by the weight of the great ripe boughs, dripping like the breasts of the earth. (*Sangre de murciélago,* 84)

In humanizing the land Godoy makes it warm, eager, and enticing. Most frequently nature is humanized as a satisfying woman, opening her arms to anguished, tired man. The sexual symbolism of the above examples is obvious. Besides spiritual unity, man may even experience a copulative union with the earth. The adjectives in the first example—long, hard, and stout —are phallic symbols, depicting the rain penetrating the brown body of earth. The presence of water heightens the sexual symbolism. The earth is a sensual haven receiving man into her heaving bosom.

Just as the earth is humanized, man becomes a part of nature. There exists in Godoy fusion and purposeful confusion. Man is not an indifferent creature, treading *on* the earth; he is a sympathetic, loving being, living *in* the earth. He returns to the earth that which he is generously given. The land is within him: "The tough commoner bent over . . . , taking a bottle of wine from the table. The wine resounded in him as if falling to an empty jug because he was made from the red clay of the land. From him oozed the soul of the people" (*Angurrientos,* 172-73).

Man, amplified with traits of nature, effects a beneficial union with the land. He learns wisdom and heroism, finds solace for his distressed soul, and unites himself with all men of his continent. Godoy does not dramatize telluric effects to the extremes of many Latin American novelists and essayists. But his men do turn to the land when rejected by women, by other men, and by society. Some elements of mysticism or fantasy pervade the union; Godoy's man is not an altogether rational, logical being. His life contains intangible as well as tangible realities. The whisperings of the land, imperceptible to much of humanity, are as real to Godoy as a wife's nagging prattle. In fact, the land may persuade more strongly than one's acquaintances. Relationships with surrounding people are limited; one man talks with another, rarely communicating feeling and spirit. Harmony with nature and earth is true communion, unlimited

by space; it joins man to the heartbeat of the universe: "He
hollowed out his bed in the warm earth and his soul merged
with the pools and the frogs in the pools, with the jugs of wine,
the worms, the red palate of the watermelon, the biting garlic . . .
all swallowed up, embraced by the land, by her hidden past;
and in his veins the heartbeat of the universe resounded like a
carpenter pounding on stout oak" (*Angurrientos*, 130-31).

Deep mysticism does not abound in Godoy's telluric theories,
nor is man's life determined by the land upon which he lives.
Unlike the characters of Naturalism of the previous century,
Godoy's men are free to choose and *become*. Natural forces are
vital and good rather than degrading. Social factors may oppress
and constrain, but nature always affords freedom and relief from
inhibition.

A vexing dilemma for man, according to Godoy, is his root-
lessness. Deserting the land, he seeks the false security of the
engulfing city. Godoy's prose is not a condemnation of city
life; he deems it necessary for one to live in community with
mankind. He does, however, censure man's alienation from the
land. He calls for a return to pristine forces; the powers from
the earth possess the capacity to extricate man and eliminate
anguish. Man need not leave the city; but while living in community, must frequently return to the timeless, untrammeled
delights of nature. He must do as Ovalle: walk a little, enjoy
the landscape, continue a moment, stop again to thrill with
nature, proceed slowly, and so forth. "This view of the countryside opened a path of bright happiness in the somber spirit of the
Sargent" (*Angurrientos*, 115). Only through regular interpene-
tration with nature will man be uplifted and simultaneously
feel ancestral, primitive forces from beneath the land. Yet only
a few of Godoy's characters are able to achieve this union.
Ovalle and Edmundo, during part of the first novel, succeed in
intercommunication. The narrator and Ordóñez in *Sangre de
murciélago* occasionally experience the soul-lifting ecstacy of
nature: an effulgent morning illuminates their souls, restoring
memories of happy, unbeguiled childhood (124). Golondrino
is most favored among Godoy's creations. Through communion
with nature he finally achieves the ultimate—power fully to control his life, death, and destiny. Though elements of fantasy
permeate Golondrino's existence, he is a conceivable being,
exemplifying the positive powers inherent in Godoy's men through

communication with nature. Golondrino "abandoned himself to the mystery, in communion with the tree, as if he too expected a blossoming of light" (*La cifra solitaria,* 67). The light arrives, and Golondrino discovers meaning and beauty in life; he is no longer rootless: "Sitting on the silver roots . . . he was filled with the spirit of the tree. . . . Shortly a sharp burning sensation as if sap of the fig tree had flooded his heart, flowed through his body, and fused the two kingdoms in a single being, still in darkness but awaiting a blossom of light" (*La cifra solitaria,* 98).

Most of Godoy's men, however, are rootless. They fail to understand self and the possibilities of telluric powers in their lives. They live in anguish, subordinated by politicians and society, protesting verbally but never acting positively. With soul-felt anxiety Horacio cries out: "We have no roots at all! We are merely instincts, powerful, wise instincts" (*Angurrientos,* 131). He challenges man to take heed, establish himself, and plant deep roots in the humus. Discovery of the sources of morality, life, and happiness will bring forth not only the complete man but the perfect society as well. Because most men are unable to live in the city and still delight in nature, they destroy themselves, through separation from the sources of strength and communication.

One of Godoy's short stories warns against rejection of civilization for complete submersion in nature. The untamed youth of "The Whip" learns of life from the land. Nature refreshes soul and body for him. His playthings are the animals from nature, while other children play with windup toys that "die" each time they run down. In his toys, "the torch of bustling life always burned, green, golden" (122). His consummate rejection of society terminates in alienation and incomprehension. At length, a wise father, who symbolically plants and cultivates domestic trees, loves the boy into accepting the values of family and society. The youth may still communicate with nature while living with mankind.

The child Eulogio receives "teeming torrents of life" from the earth. Chenda sings a "folksong which emitted the fragrance of a Chilean countryside." For Godoy, the land is the source of life. If man divorces himself from earth he amputates his soul, and life is an anguished void. The land gives roots to rootless man. It affords a concept of origins, revealing a link with the past as well as with the present. It strengthens the solitary soul, uniting it with the entire continent. The land imparts strength beyond man's own physical abilities: it purifies and pacifies, ennobles and deifies. Godoy's exquisite metaphoric symbolism illustrates earth's warm succor: "Grandma arrived! But what is a grandma? The mother of your mother. Which could easily be the land" (*Angurrientos,* 193). Man is nurtured by the mother of mothers, the fecund earth.

IV *Mythical Method*

Godoy's second means of extending the limits of man's existence is through coalescence with myth. The complex telluric relationship between man and earth expands man's spatial reality to include the entire continent. Identification with myth allows man to overstep temporal boundaries, assuming the timelessness of fable and myth. Godoy thus eliminates both the spatial and the temporal limitations of his prose; the problems dealt with are those of universal man; this is the "transition from the commonplace to the universal."

The mythical method, or as Ortega denominates it, the epic perspective, "consists of viewing the events of life as part of a few basic myths."[14] Northrop Frye similarly defines the method as "The tendency to suggest implicit mythical patterns in a world . . . closely associated with human experience."[15] A writer takes the material at hand, the *roto* (the commonplace) in Godoy's case, and links it to a long-standing myth or folkloric tradition (the universal). Hence, man of today is mythically linked with man of legend or fable. Mythical method is the basis for Joyce's *Ulysses.* Various critics have compared Godoy with Joyce, finding felicitous similarities in their prose: "I believe that Godoy attempted to do with Santiago what Joyce did with Dublin. The macrocosm is easily understood be it Chile or Ireland."[16] In Godoy, alliance with myth functions to ennoble the soul of man, bringing him closer to the gods.

A constant in Godoy's work is the mythical symbolism of wine. In excess it subverts reason, but in moderation it is exalting. Its classical function as a perpetuator of youth is seen in the story of the "Bat-blood Cure." When the victim finally learns to control his drinking, his youth is restored (89), and, in true mythical form, he lives happily ever after. Serafín, one of Godoy's most violent drinkers, is elevated by wine to an angelic state. Even his name, in Hebrew tradition, symbolizes a seraph, the highest being surrounding Jehovah's throne. Like a seraph, Serafín's symbolic wings get burned when he moves too near the light (*La cifra solitaria*, 57).

Wine also awakens virility, leads to sexual pleasure, and enhances fertility. Edmundo is a mediocre soul, but under the influence of wine he is forceful and expositive. Indulgence produces Horacio's "insatiable sexual metaphor." Wine heightens Ordóñez' virility to the point that he seeks a mistress and at least temporarily enjoys mirth and gaiety.

In mythology and folklore, wine symbolizes "consecration, elixir of eternal life, good fellowship, inspiration, refreshment, resurrection, salvation, wisdom."[17] Godoy creates an aura of myth around wine, incorporating the above connotations into his prose. Men do not gather simply to get drunk; they unite in a true bacchanal where fellowship, inspiration, and even salvation are possible. Wine permits participation in the eternities. Man becomes more than a poor Chilean when he drinks; he is a universal being, sharing in a timeless rite. Anabalón, from the first novel, is wise only when drinking (181). Wine engenders religious language, as if it were a sacred drink (*Angurrientos*, 121-24, 135, 188). Christian symbolism of wine as a purifier is also present, though infrequently. A seeming anomaly in Godoy's prose is the nondrinking Golondrino. In the author's philosophy, the blind man's abstinence would normally condemn him to a vexing terrestrial existence but his powers stem from a myth other than wine.

Related to wine is the symbolism of Bacchus and Dionysus, especially evident in the last novel. One of the characters, seized by a "mythomaniac trance," picks up a stick, which serves as a thyrsus, gives the mighty war cry of Bacchus, then calls himself Dionysus. Wine produces his mythical associations. As previously examined, sex is a recurring obsession in Godoy. Bacchus is the god of both wine and fertility. Under the influence of alcohol, man seeks woman as part of the bacchanalian rites. Wine engenders fertility in woman as well as virility in man. One of Godoy's most pitiful creations is Chocholla. Greater than the beating received from her drunken husband is the tragedy of her sterility. The problem of sterility could be solved by rendering homage to the god of fertility; but Chocholla does not drink. Her infecundity, in Godoy's world, is not tragic. It results from her willful nonconformity to myth; Godoy's wine imbues mythical powers.

The most unequivocal illustration of mythical method in Godoy is the blind Golondrino. His life and literary province in *La cifra solitaria* closely parallel the plight of Tiresias, the blind seer of ancient Greece. Two versions of the origin of Tiresias' blindness exist. The first records an argument between Zeus and Hera over the question of whether man or woman receives more pleasure from sex. They decide to ask Tiresias, who has been both man and woman. When he answers that woman does, Hera. angrily blinds him. The second version states that he accidentally came upon Athena bathing and that she blinded him. In repentance, Athena (or Zeus) compensated Tiresias with inner sight and the spirit of prophecy. This second version more nearly approaches the scope of Godoy's creation. Athena, as goddess of dawn and wisdom, imparts her powers to Tiresias. Like his mythological counterpart, Golondrino is blessed with prophecy, wisdom, and inner light. He even carries a staff, as did Tiresias, to serve as his eyes. The dog that faithfully accompanies Golondrino is Godoy's invention (and even bears the name, Brasil, of the author's pet). The symbolism surrounding Golondrino—light, roots, eyes, water— also has its base in classical tradition. To further amplify the myth, Nacha is frequently equated with light and wisdom, like Athena; she is Golondrino's spiritual daughter, imparting her light to the world.

Golondrino, the prophetic soothsayer of the village, is misunderstood and rejected by his own. The outer world is darkness; hence, he withdraws into his own light. But he is the "connecting link between reality and legend."[18] While the other characters inhabit a common, monotonous world, Golondrino overcomes limits of time and space. He attempts to bring his mythical reality to the unreceptive world. Only Loncho understands the wisdom and power of this being who transcends time. At length, Golondrino retreats from the world, and, reminiscent of Tiresias' death by water, disappears over the sea. Golondrino's prophecies, like Tiresias' seven against Thebes, live on after he departs; man must seek inner light and deep roots to avert self-destruction.

Already alluded to is the Night of San Juan, setting for *La cifra solitaria*. Usually occurring on June 24 or the summer solstice (in the Northern Hemisphere), it reverts to a pagan festival of fertility, water, and magic realization. Nacha regards her mirror as frozen water which will miraculously reveal her destiny. Rain falls continually throughout the novel, soaking the ground with life-giving moisture. On this night Satan is defeated and man is freed from demoniac powers. Golondrino sits beneath a tree in which the sap, a sign of fertility, rises from the roots and lights the branches. As a background, the Night of San Juan brings man into communication with nature, joining him with mythical tradition.

The fig tree under which Golondrino sits to gain his "spiritual light" is another link in mythical design. In Christian tradition the fig tree figures prominently in the Bible (Luke:13; Mark:11), and there are many who would make it "the tree of knowledge, the tree of good and evil."[19] The term "tree of life," also present in religious tradition, is often presumed to be the fig. As such, it denotes prolificacy and truth. In Greek mythology the fig tree is sacred to Dionysus, who derives corpulence and strength from it. Godoy incorporates all these acceptations into his second novel; Golondrino is strengthened and endowed with truth and light from the fig. As the tree sap rises, Golondrino communicates with the divine powers of the tree, which lights up as a symbol of the inner light it imparts to the blind man.

Much of the folklore previously studied joins man and myth; man is allowed beyond the bounds of his present life to participate in popular tradition. Such a technique fuses the real world with the mythical; the impossible in the real is plausible in the mythical world. The gulf between reality and folklore is bridged —all blends into an imaginative oneness. Myth does not weaken Godoy's prose but expands the horizons of man's life: "National literature is departing very rapidly from a simple naturalistic expression and new styles that capture the hidden essence of the race and its folklore, of the magic that sleeps among the masses are now invading our literature."[20]

The fanciful "Ash-colored Cock," the story of a misunderstood giant Romoán, and the "Twelve Magic Words" all unite man with mythical powers beyond the everyday world. If man loses imagination and ceases to join his life with myth and fantasy, he is doomed to misery and confinement in Godoy's world. Folklore and fantasy protract and ennoble existence.

The cockfighting motif which pervades all of *Angurrientos*

links man to myth. Besides the commoner who transforms himself into a giant cock and restores national pride, the word "cock" is itself highly symbolic. In popular jargon, a *gallo* is the commoner himself. Thus, the identification with the cock, potent and fearless, as well as with the timeless sport of cockfighting, endows man with mythical powers. The cock symbolizes "the male principle . . . , man as he was, is, and may be when he has fully realized the divinity latent within him."[21] The word is charged with significance: man is an eternal, virile being, possessed with supernatural power.

V *Conclusion*

Man, a struggling, agonizing being, fighting to raise himself from misery to decency and nobility, is the crux of Godoy's created world. Elements of style, technique, and plot revolve around and coordinate with the theme of man in affliction. The fear, inhibition, self-centeredness, and alienation which produce man's anguish and misery can be overcome only by love for others and by interiorization of self. Knowledge of one's inner self (light) and one's powerful roots will successfully elevate man from mediocrity to superiority. If he will first conquer self, he can then dominate his world. Telluric powers and union with mythical virtues simplify man's quest for a full, noble life. The world of fantasy is as real as man. When he destroys his union with that world, his life becomes oppressive and ugly. To be free from anguish, man must, according to Godoy, discover both his telluric and his mythical roots.

Intelligence must reign over fear, conformity, and irrationality. "The day will come in which the now blinded eyes of intelligence will be restored to their proper function. And then, the result will be MAN" (*Sangre de murciélago*, 36). Intelligence alone cannot raise man to nobility; it must be tempered with the warmth of intuition and love. Intelligence and intuition must work harmoniously in man; neither can dominate. If only one of these factors is operative, man is deformed and partial. Serafín, wholly intuition, twists the heads off the little pups in a drunken stupor. Ordóñez, normally a worthy example of mental balance and intelligence, bites the heads off a dozen little chicks while drinking. Thus, to free himself from distress, man must combine reason and feeling.

Godoy's theme is projected through the eyes and actions of Chilean men. From the men and minds he knows best, he draws his historical particular, endeavoring to depict the universal poetic. The idiosyncrasies of the Chilean reflect the plight of man in the contemporary world. Frequently Godoy is unable to offer solutions: life is a mystery and must simply be lived. Above good or evil, beyond anguish or joy, and more than intelligence or intuition, man must plunge wholeheartedly into the mystery of life: "I now know that in the complexity of human action, there is one permanent act, one basic concept, more or less intense, which we all feel and love and which is beyond good and evil—living."

CHAPTER 5

Juan Godoy in Chilean Literature

C RIOLLISM, the most characteristic feature of Chilean prose in the early twentieth century, has been extensively studied.[1] Far less attention has been granted to the creative movement which superseded it. The generation of 1938 remains a literary enigma to many critics. Juan Godoy pointed the initial direction and defined the essence of the new generation. His two essays, "Short Essay of the Common Man" and "Angurrientism and Culture," established the theory from which sprang the eager new generation of 1938. Since Godoy epitomizes the aims of the generation, a study of his prose, as presented in the previous chapters, also provides an understanding of the aims and accomplishments of the entire movement.

Godoy's novels and short stories manifest multiple changes from earlier literature. A major alteration is the shift from optic to haptic description. Criollistic prose is primarily based on reproducing, as faithfully as possible, the landscape, sea, or mountains. Success is equated with precise verbal duplication of nature. The novel is a photograph in words. Arturo Torres-Rioseco judges Edwards Bello's *El roto* a "photograph" of Chilean rowdies. "I use the word 'photograph' intentionally since the direct, realistic presentation of characters by Bello gives no transcendency, neither does it poeticize...."[2] Literature is methodical documentation. Conversely, Godoy extends description to include tactile, olfactory, and auditory as well as visual images. Synesthesia and complex sense imagery are also prevalent. The narrator is not an apathetic camera, but a living, feeling, integral part of the descriptive drama; the reader, too, feels an intimacy with the created world. But Godoy's merit lies not in the mere use of multiple images, rather in the precision, beauty, and accuracy of the image itself. Mere deviation from previous techniques is indicative of an innovative writer; but Godoy's graceful, exact imagery is the mark of a great artist.

The technique of Latorre and his school required a fixed landscape upon which man eventually appeared, adapted and subordinated to the created world. Social conflict was minimal or absent; man was portrayed as a conforming, regionalistic type with little transcendent interest. Again Torres-Rioseco censures this concept: "I don't feel that the role of the novel is to merely present human documentation with no more perspective than crude daily actions. Every man, simply because he is a man, when created on an artistic plane, deserves transcendent interest, intuitions, and sympathies from his author."[3] Godoy's emphasis —and that of the whole generation of 1938—is man in conflict with self and society. In Criollism physical man is sketched, living *on* the land; Godoy penetrates the spiritual man and his relationship *with* the land. As Godoy develops the soul of man in contact with nature, he endows his creations with the transcendence of universal myth and the telluric powers of the continent. In his social nonconformity and struggle for decency, man's anguished soul is of paramount concern. With deep compassion, Godoy depicts his human creations in their anxieties. Despite fears, inhibitions, and alienation, man is able to overcome inner torment through love and self-discovery. Unlike Criollism, man, not the land, is the center of Godoy's prose.

A spatial shift is also effected. The principal undertaking of former generations was a study of the countryside. To deal with problems of more universal scope, Godoy brings the scene closer to the city. But rather than lose man in the heart of the metropolis, the author portrays the cramped, poverty-ridden outskirts of Santiago, a trifling blind alley in a small town, or the disorderly community of social outcasts in an alcoholic institution. In the confinement of intimate city life, man's soul is more easily bared. His problems are not merely those of a Chilean but those of man in all cities of the world.

Essentially, action is the governing precept of Criollism and earlier literary thought. Orderly, often episodic, development in time and space is requisite to novelistic form. In Godoy, action revolves in concentric patterns, with little spatial or temporal progression. That which was previously considered accessory and embellishment—language, metaphor, and poetry— supplant action. If a man's inner feelings can be revealed instantaneously through an appropriate symbol, Godoy will do so, rather than belabor the conflict over an extended period. Action is secondary to poetic intensity. As in Alejo Carpentier, María Luisa Bombal, Juan Rulfo, and other Latin American contemporaries, lyric expression of human problems supersedes plot development. Godoy achieves poetic intensity through countless devices: archaic words and syntax, prose rhythm, onomatopoeia, alliteration, sensual images, synesthesia, and, most important, original metaphors.

Godoy bases his prose on metaphor. Criollism describes the real, commonplace world in straightforward, logical terminology. A writer is successful when he captures an image through direct, concise description. Language portrays the real world, much as a camera or tape recorder would reproduce it. Godoy's significant shift to metaphoric expression enriches creation by merging two worlds—the real and the comparative. The everyday world of reality is given depth and meaning by implication and comparison. As Godoy describes nature, for example, he imbues it with human qualities. Beautiful to behold, nature is also alive and personal. Man is described as powerful and active, and he is further exalted through metaphoric comparison with the sea. Thus, the levels of reality and comparison unite in Godoy to create highly poetic prose. Among stylistic techniques in Godoy's prose, metaphor is most distinctive. Complex metaphoric technique set Godoy apart from the previous literary movement and, in fact, from many of his own generation. Unless the reader fully comprehends the author's metaphors, titles of the novels, chapter titles, character delineation, human relationships, and even syntax will appear jumbled and meaningless. A complete grasp of Godoy's metaphors is difficult, requiring complete submersion in the work. The casual, on-and-off reader will derive little pleasure from the prose.

Literature based on metaphor and poetic expression is regarded by many critics as the new style in prose.[4] It is the element which raises Godoy's first novel from mere Naturalistic documentation to the more abstract realms of universality. Style for Godoy is not the faithful reproduction of the surrounding world; rather, it is the addition of a fourth dimension to life, through metaphoric poetization and intuition of reality.

A further departure from Criollism, and a step in the direction of poetry, is Godoy's method of creation and development. Unlike orderly narrative progression, Godoy creates spontaneous, often hybrid narrative, which closely parallels the gratuitous, lyric outburst of the poet. "Regarding inspiration, the prose poem derives from the creative mind of the poet. It uses the techniques of poetry.... And, logically, it should explore the least expected and obvious aspects of each object."[5] In Godoy, unexpected poetic expression produces the "stamp," an atemporal lyric picture, which stands out from narrative development. The author revels in poetry; the "stamps" contain Godoy's most graceful images and metaphors. Instead of the temporal evolution of the traditional novel, Godoy creates the instantaneity of poetry. Angurrientism, as envisioned by Godoy, is the "*intuition of cultural essence.*" Intuition is not rational and orderly but irrational and choppy; it is the revelation of the latent poetry in man's soul. The active elements of prose are transformed to contemplative, human, or natural drama in Godoy, and the poetic "stamp" supplants narrative description.

The writer's man-centered symbols—the ox, sea, sky, roots, light, ashes, wine, mirror—emphasize the poetic universal nature of man, in contrast to the regionalistic character types of Criollism. Godoy ignores regional and national barriers and encompasses all mankind. Through symbolism, association with poetic myth, and telluric identification, Godoy's men are molded into universal figures. On the symbolic level there is undeviating movement toward light. Godoy's men, just as men everywhere, are searching for the truth and knowledge that will light their lives.

The Latin American novel has undergone severe criticism for its lack of universality. The literature has been censured for its nationalistic characters, its limited spatial development, its foundation in regionalistic terms, and its divorce from the mother tongue. Also under criticism has been its excessive poetry, its paltry dramatic qualities, its emphasis on the land and country rather than on the city.[6] While Godoy may be "guilty" of some of these literary "sins," he has conscientiously sought for universality and unlimited application. His characters endure the anguish not only of the Chilean Angurrientist but of all mankind. His denunciation of alcoholism echoes throughout the world. Although the bulk of his diction is current Spanish, his prose is studded with Chilean and American terms. These, however, fulfill purposes greater than universality in their contribution to precision and enrichment. To assure comprehension of these terms, he frequently supplies sufficient definition in the context of the prose or includes a glossary to explain difficult terminology. Concurrent with regionalisms Godoy employs Golden Age language to enrich poetic flavor and aid precision. Such language does not hinder universality.

Neither can Godoy be seriously accused of excessive poetry. His poetry is excessive only when measured against poetic content in another century or movement. Within the bounds of Godoy's created world, poetry is a necessity rather than an accessory. It deepens meaning in the prose, elevating the novel from artless description of sordid life to a far-reaching, compassionate understanding of humanity.

Internal participating narrators heighten drama. There is an everpresent tendency to postpone outcome, thus creating suspense. Imagery is used to increase dramatic tension, obvious in the frightful death wake of *La cifra solitaria*. While Godoy does establish a relationship with man and nature, this in no way confines the scope of the novel. To the contrary, it broadens man's world, making him part of a continental unity. Man is neither determined nor shaped by his land; he merely derives strength from it—if he so chooses. The city, with its unanswered problems for all mankind, is the arena for Godoy's prose. Through careful selection and development of the historic particular, Godoy reaches a significant universal poetic: man in anguish.

Godoy takes daily life and transfigures it. He peels off anecdotal aspects . . . his creative spirit gives form to life beyond our five senses, in hidden regions where esoteric investigations discover a net of anguish.

Therefore we must distinguish between two aspects of Godoy: the writer who marks new paths for Chilean prose and the artist who joins the current of world literature as a result of universal content.

Chile provides Godoy its tattered beings. The creator fashions new beings, gives them new life, transfigures them, and converts them into teeming, universal men.[7]

Juan Godoy has been eulogized as "the most poetic of Chilean writers."[8] Whether this honor is virtue or vice is hotly debated in Chile. Raúl Pinto Cortínez considers Godoy a sad poet, shipwrecked on the sandy beaches of prose.[9] In the main, however, Chilean and Latin American critics praise Godoy's work. While delving into human tribulation and social oppression, he frees himself from the vulgarity of Naturalistic expression through elevated stylistic resources. Instead of adhering to traditional novelistic formulas, he has brought innovation to the genre. Godoy is, and will be, remembered as a great stylist. At the same time, he is an excellent novelist; his sympathetic portrayal of universal human struggle is as well wrought as his style.

Wayne Booth examines three types of interest levels a reader may experience in a work of art: the first, intellectual interest, is derived from causal completion, balance, symmetry, comparison, and so on; the second is practical interest, a strong concern in the reader for the characters as people; the third is esthetic interest.[10] The greatness of Godoy's prose stems from its harmonious appeal to all three interest levels. The author creates a richness rare in Chilean prose. Interest levels blend in a single work of polished art. Although Juan Godoy, "the greatest author of his generation," has not produced the great Latin American novel of which critics felt him capable, his complex prose gravitates so close to that pinnacle as to warrant continual reading and serious criticism.

Notes and References

Chapter One

1. *Estampas del nuevo extremo: Antología de Santiago*: 1541-1941 (Santiago, 1941), p. xlvii.
2. "New Currents in Chilean Fiction," *Americas*, I (October, 1949), 40.
3. *La novela hispanoamericana* (Santiago, 1963), p. 337.
4. "*Sangre de murciélago*, por Juan Godoy," *Clarín* (Santiago, January 10, 1960).
5. The sources of information for this brief biography, unless otherwise noted, were provided by Juan Godoy himself or by members of his family whom the writer interviewed during his visit to Santiago in November and December, 1966.
6. Felipe Delta, "*Angurrientos*, novela por Juan Godoy," *Los libros por dentro* (Santiago, April 13, 1941).
7. Interview with Yolando Pino Saavedra, October 31, 1966, Los Angeles, California.
8. Personal interview with César Búnster, November 30, 1966, Santiago.
9. Pablo de Rokha, "*Sangre de murciélago*, por Juan Godoy," *Multitud*, LXXXVII (1959), 20.
10. Jorge Jobet, "*Sangre de murciélago*, novela de Juan Godoy," *Atenea*, CXXXVII:387 (1960), 154.
11. Mario Ferrero, "Caleidoscopio del Premio Nacional de Literatura," *Portal*, III (1966), 7.
12. "Algo sobre la creación literaria," *Boletín del Instituto Nacional*, LXIV (1960), 32.
13. Eleazar Huerta, "*La cifra solitaria*," *Las Ultimas Noticias* [Crónica de libros] (Santiago, December 20, 1952).
14. Interview with Juan Godoy, November 18, 1966, Santiago, Chile.
15. Interview with Juan Godoy, November 26, 1966, Santiago, Chile.
16. Interview with Yolando Pino Saavedra, January 6, 1967, Los Angeles, California.
17. Gladis Thein, "*La cifra solitaria*," *Boletín del Instituto Nacional*, XXV (1946), 36.
18. Jorge Jobet, "*Sangre de murciélago*, novela de Juan Godoy," *Atenea*, CXXXVII:387 (1960), 159.

19. José Juan Arrom, *Esquema generacional de las letras hispano-americanas: Ensayo de un método* (Bogota, 1963), p. 195.

20. "Nuevas consideraciones sobre la novela chilena," *Papeles de Son Armadans*, XXXIII (1964), 15.

21. "Resolución de medio siglo," *Atenea*, CXXXI:380-81 (1958), 141-48.

22. "La generación del '38 en busca de la realidad chilena," *Atenea*, CXXXI:380-81 (1958), 115.

23. Juan Godoy, *Sangre de murciélago* (Santiago, 1959), pp. 139-40.

24. Felipe Delta, *"Angurrientos*, novela por Juan Godoy," *Los libros por dentro* (Santiago, April 13, 1941).

25. Mario Espinosa, "Una generación," *Atenea*, CXXXI:380-81 (1958), 73.

26. Victor M. Valenzuela, "A New Generation of Chilean Novelists and Short Story Writers," *Hispania*, XXXVIII:4 (1954), 440.

27. Fernando Alegría, *Las fronteras del realismo, literatura chilena del siglo XX* (Santiago, 1962), p. 116.

28. Luis Alberto Sánchez, *"Angurrientos*, por Juan Godoy," *Hoy* (Santiago, December 26, 1940).

29. Notably, Pedro Lastra Salazar of the Institute of Chilean Literature, Santiago, Chile, who gave me invaluable assistance in delineating the various facets of the generation of 1938.

30. In an interview with Juan Godoy, November 16, 1966, he emphatically stated that Neruda was doing nothing more than using Angurrientismo in his "Apogee of Celery" and "Statute of Wine."

31. "Angurrientismo y cultura," *Aurora de Chile*, XIII (August 4, 1939), 4.

32. Manuel Rojas, in his 1926 *Hombres del Sur* had hinted at the same concept, "El Bonete Maulino," but did not develop it fully.

33. Martín Alonso, *Enciclopedia del Idioma* (Madrid, 1958), p. 364.

34. Victor M. Valenzuela, "A New Generation of Chilean Novelists and Short Story Writers," *Hispania*, XXXVII:4 (1954), 411.

35. Enrique Anderson Imbert, *Spanish-American Literature. A History*, trans. John V. Falconieri (Detroit, 1963), p. 504.

36. Ricardo A. Latcham, "New Currents in Chilean Fiction," *Americas*, I:8 (1949), 40.

37. Julio Durán Cerda, *"Angurrientos* por Juan Godoy," *Boletín del Instituto Nacional*, IX (1941), 40.

38. Domingo Melfi, *"Angurrientos*, novela por Juan Godoy," *La Nación*, Santiago, March 30, 1941.

39. "Angurrientismo y cultura," *Aurora de Chile*, XIII (August 4, 1939), 4.

40. Interview with Juan Godoy, November 20, 1966, Santiago. This is not intended to be a complete list of the authors who wrote

in the Angurrientist style; it is compiled from the memory of Juan Godoy and may exclude some who considered themselves members of the group.

41. Interview, November 20, 1966, Santiago. Godoy views his role as one of an initiator who united individual, aspiring writers into a group and gave them their first ideological push. After this start they found their own styles and themes.

42. Arnold Chapman, "Perspectiva de la novela de la ciudad," *La novela iberoamericana,* ed. Torres-Rioseco (Albuquerque, 1952), p. 200.

43. *Historia de las literaturas de vanguardia* (Madrid, 1965), p. 774.

44. Again, I am indebted to Guillermo de Torre, pp. 766-84, for his summary study of the movement and its identifying features.

45. De Torre, p. 779.

46. Adolf Ramírez, "The Chilean Novel of Social Protest," Ph.D. dissertation (University of Wisconsin, 1956), pp. vii, 159.

47. Luis Merino Reyes, "La generación del 38," *Portal* 3 (1966), 14.

Chapter Two

1. Interview with Juan Godoy, December 2, 1966, Santiago, Chile.

2. Luis Durand, "La mitología chilena y sus leyendas," *Presencia de Chile* (Santiago, 1942), p. 27.

3. Interview with Elisa Godoy de Rojas, August 28, 1968, Santiago, Chile.

Chapter Three

1. William K. Wimsatt, Jr., *The Prose Style of Samuel Johnson* (New Haven, 1941), pp. 3-4.

2. Lina Schälchly, *Juan Godoy, ensayo de interpretación estilística,* unpublished "Memoria" (University of Chile, 1955), p. 147.

3. *La literatura chilena* (Buenos Aires, 1941), p. 92.

4. Raúl Pinto Cortínez, "A caza de un autor," *Hoy,* Santiago, March 6, 1949.

5. Enrique Anderson Imbert (*¿Qué es la prosa?* [Buenos Aires, 1958], pp. 23, 24) lists sixteen types from allusion to synecdoche. Other critics have even further proliferated categories.

6. If Neruda's symbolism is accepted here, this too is an ennobling comparison: *Abejas son símbolo del ardor de la vida, del frenesí amoroso o báquico o dionisíaco.* Amado Alonso, *Poesía y estilo de Pablo Neruda* (Buenos Aires, 1951), p. 217.

7. Amado Alonso, *Poesía y estilo de Pablo Neruda* (Buenos Aires, 1951), pp. 262-66. Man's anguish and symbols that represent it are studied in the chapter on theme.

8. Pedro Selva, "Una epidemia literaria," *Atenea*, LXXXIII:249 (1946), 416.

9. Marjorie Boulton, *The Anatomy of Prose* (London, 1954), p. 151.

10. For the initial classification of Godoy's symbols, I am deeply indebted to Lina Schälchly's study, pp. 93-111. To her study I have added several other symbols, resulting from the author's later novels and short stories.

11. Pablo García, "Aporte para la interpretación estética de Juan Godoy," *Atenea*, XCIV:289-90 (1949), 199.

12. The alliterative "Ronca corriente subterranea . . ." strengthens the symbolic idea of "*raíces*."

13. This symbolic use of the sea parallels Neruda's symbolism in the already cited Angurrientist poems "Apogeo del Apio" and "Estatuto del Vino" as well as "Barcarola," "Madrigal escrito en invierno," and "Lamento lento." Amado Alonso, *Poesía y estilo de Pablo Neruda* (Buenos Aires, 1951), pp. 264-68.

14. Arnold Chapman, "Perspectiva de la novela de la ciudad en Chile," *La Novela Iberoamericana*, ed. Arturo Torres-Rioseco (Albuquerque, New Mexico), p. 204.

15. Northrop Frye, *Anatomy of Criticism* (Princeton, New Jersey, 1957), p. 115.

16. Norman Friedman, "Point of View in Fiction: The Development of a Critical Concept," *PMLA*, LXX:5 (1955), 1169-74.

17. Wayne C. Booth, *The Rhetoric of Fiction*, 5th ed. (Chicago, 1965), p. 151.

18. Godoy sees no loss of unity, since he considers the novel to be autobiographical, with himself as both narrators. (Interview, November 20, 1966, Santiago.) This may be true but is an extraliterary source, not inherent in the novel itself.

19. Booth, p. 158.

20. Benjamín Rojas Piña, "Dos comentarios a *Sangre de murciélago*," *Boletín del Instituto Nacional*, LXI and LXII (1959), 15.

21. Raúl Pinto Cortínez, "A caza de un autor," *Hoy*, Santiago, March 6, 1949.

22. Marta Brunet, "Carta para Juan Godoy," *Boletín del Instituto Nacional*, XXVIII (1947), 31.

23. Raúl Silva Castro, for example, chooses to call *Angurrientos* "una sucesión de cuadros . . . ," *Historia Crítica de la novela chilena* (Madrid, 1960), 378. Cruchaga and other critics have adopted similar terminology.

24. Eleazar Huerta, "*La cifra solitaria*," *Las Ultimas Noticias* [Crónica de libros] (Santiago, December 7, 1945).

25. "*Angurrientos*, novela por Juan Godoy," *La Nación* [Crónica de libros] (Santiago, March 30, 1941).

26. Luis Alvaro Droguett, "Boceto sobre Juan Godoy," *Pro Arte*, Santiago, December 7, 1950.

27. Mariano Baquero Goyanes, *Prosistas españoles contemporáneos* (Madrid, 1956), pp. 179-90.

28. Guillermo Diaz-Plaja, *El poema en prosa en España* (Barcelona, 1956), p. 22.

29. Ricardo Benavides Lillo, "*Angurrientos* de Juan Godoy," *La Libertad* [Crítica literaria] (Santiago, December 28, 1959).

30. Jorge Jobet, "*Sangre de murciélago,* novela de Juan Godoy," *Atenea,* CXXXVII:387 (1960), 160.

31. Hans Meyerhoff, *Time in Literature* (Berkeley and Los Angeles, 1955), p. 4.

32. A. A. Mendilow, *Time and the Novel* (Deventer, Holland, 1952), p. 106.

33. Edwin Muir, *The Structure of the Novel* (London, 1938), p. 42.

34. Interview with Yolando Pino Saavedra, Los Angeles, California, November 11, 1966.

35. Luis Durand, "La mitología chilena y sus leyendas," *Presencia de Chile* (Santiago, 1942), p. 40.

36. Reinaldo Lomboy, "Juan Godoy se desdibuja (El hombre y la palabra)," *Zig-Zag,* Santiago, September 22, 1956.

37. Enrique Anderson Imbert, *Historia de la literatura hispanoamericana* (Mexico, 1954), p. 382.

38. Volodia Teitelboim, "*La cifra solitaria,*" *El siglo* [Comentario de libros y autores] (Santiago, December 23, 1945).

Chapter Four

1. Volodia Teitelboim, "La generación del 38 en busca de la realidad chilena," *Atenea,* CXXXI:380-81 (1958), 120.

2. Alberto Zum Felde, *La Narrativa en Hispanoamérica* (Madrid, 1964), p. 10.

3. Enrique Anderson Imbert, "Spanish-American Literature in the Last Twenty-five Years," *Books Abroad,* XXVII (1953), 357.

4. Fernando Alegría, "The Changing Spanish-American Novel," *Americas,* VIII (March, 1956), 42.

5. François Meyer, *La ontología de Miguel de Unamuno* (Madrid, 1962), p. 31.

6. *Ibid.*

7. Jorge Jobet, "*Sangre de murciélago,* novela de Juan Godoy," *Atenea,* CXXXVII:387 (1960), 158.

8. Fernando Alegría appears to have been the first; Enrique Anderson Imbert and others have followed suit. Alegría states: "*La verdad es que Godoy es un discípulo del unanimismo francés y en Jules Romains aprendió las primeras armas de su transcendentalismo popular.*" *Las fronteras del realismo* (Santiago, 1962), p. 118.

9. Yerko Moretíc, "*Sangre de murciélago*, de Juan Godoy," *Atenea*, CXXXV:385 (1959), 203.

10. Nicomedes Guzmán, *Nuevos cuentistas chilenos* (Santiago, 1941), pp. 14-15. Arnold Chapman, Hugo Montes Brunet, and Raúl Silva Castro have only seen tragic man in Godoy, caught between sex and alcohol.

11. Various critics, however, have seen Godoy's creations as predestined and controlled by fate: "*El hombre es un juguete en las manos de un destino de origen desconocido*," Sergio Latorre V., "El gato de la maestranza," *Las Noticias de Ultima Hora* [Crónica de libros] (Santiago, November 11, 1952).

12. Luis Droguett Alvaro, "*La cifra solitaria*, de Juan Godoy," *La Nación*, Santiago, December 30, 1945.

13. Interview with Juan Godoy, November 27, 1966, Santiago, Chile.

14. José Ortega y Gasset, *Meditaciones del Quijote, Obras Completas*, 5th ed. (Madrid, 1961), 376.

15. *Anatomy of Criticism* (Princeton, New Jersey, 1957), pp. 139-40.

16. Arnold Chapman, "Perspectiva de la novela de la ciudad en Chile," *La Novela Iberoamericana*, ed. Arturo Torres-Rioseco (Albuquerque, New Mexico, 1952), p. 204.

17. Gertrude Jobes, *Mythology, Folklore and Symbols*, II (New York, 1961), 1684.

18. Benjamín Rojas Piña, "*Cifra solitaria*, por Juan Godoy," *Atenea*, CL:399 (1963), 222.

19. Pablo García," Aporte para la interpretación estética de Juan Godoy," *Atenea*, XCIV:289-90 (1949), 201.

20. Ricardo A. Latcham, "*La cifra solitaria*," *La Nación* [Crónica literaria] (Santiago, November 25, 1945).

21. Gertrude Jobes, *Mythology, Folklore and Symbols*, I (New York, 1961), 353.

Chapter Five

1. Compare Homero Castillo, *El criollismo en la novelística chilena* (Mexico, 1962); Domingo Melfi, *Estudios de literatura chilena* (Santiago, 1938); and Manuel Vega, Ernesto Montenegro, and Ricardo Latcham, *El criollismo* (Santiago, 1956).

2. "Nuevas consideraciones sobre la novela chilena," *Papeles de Son Armadans*, XXXIII:97 (1964), 13.

3. *Ibid.*

4. Arturo Torres-Rioseco, "El nueva estilo en la novela," *Revista Iberoamericana*, III:5 (1941), 75.

5. Guillermo Diaz-Plaja, *El poema en prosa en España* (Barcelona, 1956), p. 22.

6. Uriel Ospina, *Problemas y perspectivas de la novela americana* (Bogota, 1964), pp. 221-23; Alberto Zum Felde, *La Narrativa en Hispanoamérica* (Madrid, 1964), pp. 10-14.

7. Pablo García, "Aporte para la interpretación estética de Juan Godoy," *Atenea*, XCIV:289-90 (1949), 198.

8. Jorge Jobet, "*Sangre de murciélago*, novela de Juan Godoy," *Atenea*, CXXXVII:387 (1960), 156.

9. "A caza de un autor," *Hoy*, Santiago, March 6, 1949.

10. Wayne C. Booth, *The Rhetoric of Fiction* (Chicago, 1965), pp. 125-33.

Selected Bibliography

PRIMARY SOURCES

1. Creative works

Angurrientos (Santiago: Escuela Nacional de Artes Gráficas, 1940).
————— (Santiago: Nascimento, 1959).
La cifra solitaria (Santiago: Escuela Nacional de Artes Gráficas, 1945).
Cifra solitaria (Santiago: Escuela Industrial de Artes Gráficas, 1962).
El gato de la maestranza y otros cuentos (Santiago: Escuela Nacional de Artes Gráficas, 1952).
"L'Herminia se ha vengao." *Nuevos cuentistas chilenos,* compiled by Nicomedes Guzmán (Santiago Ediciones "Cultura," 1941).
El impedido (Santiago: Ediciones Quenaci, 1968).
"Un inspector de sanidad . . . o cómo un alto dignatario murió en sus manos" (Santiago: Escuela Nacional de Artes Gráficas, 1950).
"La lengua del buey." *Boletín del Instituto Nacional* (Santiago), VI: 11 (November, 1950), 23.
Sangre de murciélago (Santiago: Prensa Latinoamericana, 1959).
"Sombras." *Mapocho* (Santiago), V:1 (1966), 50-52.

2. Critical works

"Algo sobre la creación literaria." *Bolétin del Instituto Nacional* (Santiago), LXIV (March, 1960), 32.
"Angurrientismo y cultura." *Aurora de Chile* [Santiago], XIII (August, 1939), 4-5.
"Breve ensayo sobre el roto." *Atenea,* LV:163 (1939), 33-40.
"Mi punto de partida." *Bolétin del Instituto Nacional* (Santiago), LIX (July-September, 1958), 33.

SECONDARY SOURCES

Critical Appraisals of Juan Godoy and the Generation of 1938

ALEGRÍA, FERNANDO. *Las fronteras del realismo. Literatura chilena del siglo XX* (Santiago: Zig-Zag, 1962). An excellent study providing background and analysis for the entire century. Godoy is studied in context with his contemporaries.

──────. "Resolución de medio siglo," *Atenea*, CXXXI:380-81 (1958), 141-48. Short examination of the influences operating on the generation of 1938, as seen by one of its own members.

CHAPMAN, ARNOLD. "Observations on the 'roto' in Chilean Fiction," *Hispania*, XXXII:3 (1949), 309-14. The best study available to a wide public on the *roto* as a type in Chilean literature.

DURÁN CERDA, JULIO. "*Angurrientos*, por Juan Godoy," *Bolétin del Instituto Nacional* [Santiago], IX (May, 1941), 28-34. The most detailed and accurate analysis of Godoy's first novel, relating it to the Chilean scene it reflects.

ESPINOSA, MARIO. "Una generación," *Atenea*, CXXXI:380-81 (1958), 66-77. A summary study of the groupings into generations of literature in Chile.

GARCÍA, PABLO. "Aporte para la interpretación estética de Juan Godoy," *Atenea*, XCIV:289-90 (1949), 197-202. Although the study does not include the author's last two novels and short stories, it provides an excellent stylistic analysis of his prose.

LOMBOY, REINALDO. "Juan Godoy se desdibuja (El hombre y la palabra)," *Zig-Zag* (Santiago), September 22, 1956. A brief but valuable narrative of the author's life experience as it relates to his prose.

MERINO REYES, LUIS. "La generación del 38," *Portal* (Santiago), III (July, 1966), 14. A very personal view of the formation of the generation of 1938, overlooking Godoy as an important figure of the group.

OYARZÚN, LUIS. "Crónica de una generación," *Atenea*, CXXXI:380-81 (1958), 180-89. A detailed but subjective analysis of literary factors which influenced the creation of the generation of 1938.

SABELLA, ANDRÉS. "Estilo y sugestión en Juan Godoy," *Las Ultimas Noticias*, Santiago, June 13, 1946). The first serious study pointing out specific tendencies of poetic narration in Godoy's prose.

SCHÄLCHLY, LINA. "Juan Godoy, ensayo de interpretación estilística," unpublished doctoral thesis in the Instituto Pedagógico de la Universidad de Chile, 1955, directed by Eleazar Huerta. A thorough, formalistic study of Godoy's prose to 1955. The author is number conscious and often bogs down in description rather than analysis and interpretation of the literature.

──────. "Noticia biográfica de Juan Godoy." Prologue to *Sangre de murciélago*, 1959. A short essay on the life of the author, somewhat subjectively viewed.

TEITELBOIM, VOLODIA. "La generación del 38 en busca de la realidad chilena," *Atenea*, CXXXI:380-81 (1959), 106-31. A detailed, innovative approach to the goals promulgated by the generation it describes.

Index